YPSILANTI GHOSTS & LEGENDS

CRYSTA K. COBURN AND KAY GRAY

Published by Haunted America
A Division of The History Press
Charleston, SC
www.historypress.com

Cover image: The Ypsilanti Water Tower, with statue of Demetrious Ypsilanti. *Kay Gray*.

First published 2024

Manufactured in the United States

ISBN 9781467158091

Library of Congress Control Number: 2024937648

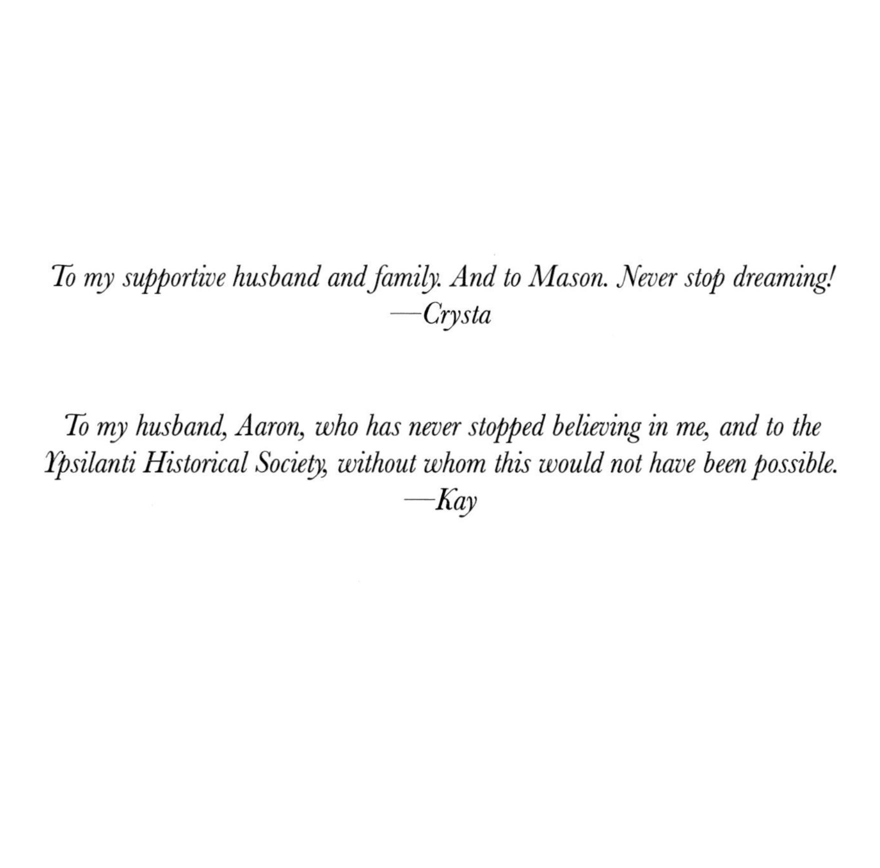

To my supportive husband and family. And to Mason. Never stop dreaming!
—Crysta

To my husband, Aaron, who has never stopped believing in me, and to the Ypsilanti Historical Society, without whom this would not have been possible.
—Kay

CONTENTS

INTRODUCTION

In the preindustrial times, what is now Washtenaw County, Michigan, with the sizable Huron River offering easy access to the Great Lakes, was first-rate living and home to a number of American Indian tribes such as the Odawa, Ojibwe, Potawatomi and Wyandot. The river itself was once known as Nottawaseppi (River of the Hurons) in Algonquian and Giwitatigweiasibi (Burnt-Oak Region) in Huron.

Now nestled between the bustling college town of Ann Arbor and the Motor City, Ypsilanti often gets overlooked as a destination of any kind, much less the paranormal variety. But it has been around since the French fur trapping days of Michigan's past and was the first documented settlement in Washtenaw County. Back in 1823, the little settlement clustered around what is now the junction of South Prospect and South Grove streets was named Woodruff's Grove, after settler Benjamin Woodruff, and existed as a small waystation between Chicago and Detroit along the Chicago Road. A historical marker exists at the site today, placed there in 1923 by the Ypsilanti Chapter of the Daughters of the American Revolution.

The actual Huron River crossing for the road was made one mile north of Woodruff's Grove. Another community sprang up around it and was named Ypsilanti in honor of General Demetrios Ypsilantis, a hero of the War of Greek Independence (1821–32). A bust of Ypsilantis stands adjacent to the infamous Water Tower just to the west of today's Depot Town. The settlement of Ypsilanti gained prominence, and populations shifted north, when a fire at the Woodruff's Grove school led to that community's decline.

Many of Ypsilanti's old buildings are reported to be haunted by spirits of the past. The oldest home still standing on its original foundation in Washtenaw County is located on North Huron Street in Ypsilanti. It was built in the Greek Revival style in 1837 and is known today as the Towner House. Eastern Michigan University was established in 1849, and its oldest still-standing building, Starkweather Hall, was opened in 1896. Does a woman in old-fashioned clothing roam its halls? The Michigan Firehouse Museum incorporates the beautifully maintained original 1898 firehouse building, where a former fire chief might still be at his post. And while it was constructed in the mid-twentieth century, the Willow Run Airport has its fair share of stories as well.

Ghost stories aside, Ypsilanti is full of legends too. The young city was a critical stop for countless freedom seekers who traveled the Underground Railroad. Depot Town's below-ground tunnels may have provided a safe place to hide during the day, while the Huron River offered safer passage at night. Nearly one hundred years later, there were the Three Christs of Ypsilanti at the now-closed Ypsilanti State Hospital. And who could forget the infamous UFO flap of 1966 that led to the highly questionable swamp gas theory? Or John Norman Collins's reign of terror?

In the following pages, you will learn about all of these tales and more. And you may never see Ypsilanti the same way again.

A NOTE ON INVESTIGATING THE PARANORMAL

In the world of the paranormal, there are several items, words and phrases that are used often but perhaps rarely explained to those who are new to the field or popping in from other fields and areas of interest. Let this act as the guide for the rest of the book.

First, this book uses a wide variety of terms for what are commonly referred to as "ghosts." Entities, spirits, hauntings, specters, apparitions, ghosts, beings and presences are all mentioned within this book to describe what people are interacting with in their businesses and homes. While not everyone agrees that these are all the same thing, including the authors, using more descriptors than just "ghost" allows for a broader definition for what is active in these buildings than simply "the dead."

Generally speaking, while there are definitions for "ghosts" and "spirits," there is no consensus on what they really are, nor any definitive, tried-and-true way of finding out. Ghosts could be the souls of the dead still wandering Earth for reasons of their own. They could be living people in their own time, and time has overlapped somehow (this book will refer to that as a "time slip"). These beings may not even be from this plane of existence at all but rather are visitors from somewhere humans can scarcely imagine. This could all be some sort of psychic phenomenon the human brain is designed to make up. They could be all of these things or none of these things.

A catch-all term used frequently within paranormal circles is "high strangeness." This is generally used to describe something out of the ordinary that maybe can't be sorted into a neat category. A.P. Strange—paranormal researcher, author and podcaster—frames "high strangeness" like so:

> *High strangeness can loosely be defined as an event or series of events that defies the commonly accepted natural order of Things, and in the modern study of the unexplained is often reserved for the weirdest of the weird stories. Owing its etymological lineage to Dr. J. Allen Hynek, who is known for his UFO "Close Encounters" Scale, the strangeness factor was similarly a method of measuring and classifying a reported experience. Events that scored low on the strangeness scale were relatively easy to address with probable prosaic explanations; more complicated reports, however, were not so easily dispatched.*

People who experience things that cannot easily be explained away scientifically often do not talk about them, fearing what others will think. Did it really happen? Or are they delusional? A.P. Strange goes on to point out that some incidents "defy easy categorization. High strangeness, then, can be defined as a story simply too weird to be true, but so far as can be determined, is."

And that's where the "investigation" part comes in. Those in the paranormal field of study try to interact with whatever ghosts are for any number of reasons, just a few of which are to find out if they are real (and not, for example, hoaxes), if they can communicate with humans and/or to help these entities get what they need to find peace. Some people want to dive into extremely strange stories just because. But there are myriad reasons investigators have for trying to contact spirits, ranging from the deeply personal to the clinically scientific.

Also, let it be said that not all paranormal investigations are the same. Some people like to call it "ghost hunting," others use "investigation" and there are those out there who prefer to think of their time with the unknown as a conversation or a meeting. Some investigations are done with all the latest technology in the paranormal world, and some are done with nothing but a person's own intuition, emotions and voice. As long as no harm is being done to either party (paranormal or human), all ways of investigation are valid and useful to the field of paranormal study.

Investigations use a wide range of gadgets to try to capture evidence of the unknown. In this book, audio recorders are heavily featured. They are used often in recording "electronic voice phenomena," otherwise known as EVP. The theory is that spirits may not be able to make themselves heard out loud, but they can talk through audio devices both analogue and digital. So while an investigator may not hear a response to a question in the moment, the spirit may have left an answer that can only be heard upon playing back the recording.

Cameras are another big item in some investigations. An investigator may not see something with their own eyes, but a photo or video could show a black mass, a strange mist or other such anomalies that might be evidence of a presence. These days, a lot of groups try their hand at an SLS camera, which originated from the Xbox's Kinect device and which records movements and translates them to the program or game on screen. SLS translates to "structured light 3D scanner." The idea is that the SLS will pick up any human-shaped form (i.e., a ghost) and will translate that on screen as a stick figure. Investigators can use this as evidence that a presence is near them. However, it must be noted that the SLS camera has been controversial ever since it arrived on the scene. Use with caution.

Other common devices used in plenty of television and other investigations include electromagnetic field detectors (EMF), which are actually home repair tools that detect the level of electric and magnetic fields in the air in a small area. The theory is that spirits may use these fields to gain energy to materialize and that a high reading could mean one is nearby. REM pods have become more and more common. They are small devices that radiate the electromagnetic field themselves, possibly aiding the entity in manifesting. Both of these are often used while an investigator asks yes or no questions. "Come closer to the device for a yes, stay away for no."

The last device mentioned with any regularity in this book is the thermal camera. Another home repair tool, the thermal camera senses temperature and translates that to a small screen by showing the world in different colors representing varying degrees of heat. There has been a long-held theory that ghosts use heat to gain energy to manifest. If an area on the screen is abnormally colder or hotter than everything around it, there may be a spirit there. (It's also useful in finding where heat is being lost in a house.)

There are so many more gadgets out there that supposedly help investigators make contact with the paranormal that it would be a chapter on its own just to name them all. Suffice it to say that investigators use anything and everything in the toolbox, experimenting with new technology, old technology and their own bodies for the sake of contact. The paranormal field is nothing if not innovative.

Are any of these a requirement in paranormal investigation? Absolutely not. One of the best things about the field is that nearly every approach is valid (those investigators who choose to aggressively provoke aside…). However one wants to explore the paranormal is welcome. Not everyone can afford hundreds of dollars of equipment, and not everyone has to. Not everyone can visit giant, abandoned asylums, and not everyone has to. There is room for all at the haunted table. The more the merrier. Let this book be the guide to one small section of this wide, spooky world. Enjoy the ride.

Part I
Downtown

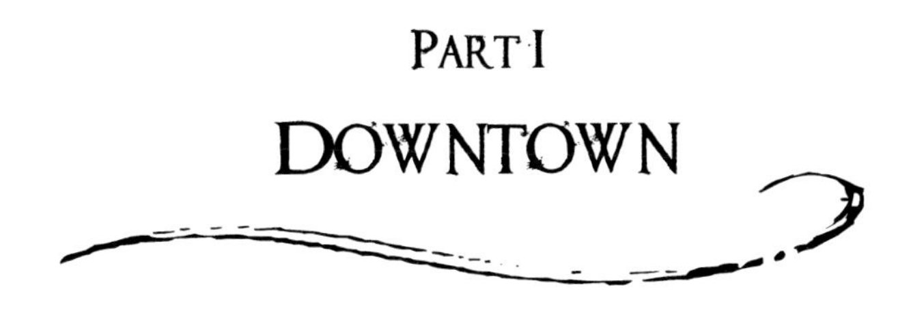

YPSILANTI DISTRICT LIBRARY

The Ladies Library

Heading north on Huron Street is akin to stepping back in time. The homes and offices and churches lining the stretch between Michigan Avenue and Forest Avenue are all at least one hundred years old, and most of them have been either well preserved or restored to look their best. One such building, a brick Italianate beauty, claims in stone that it is the Ladies Library. (Yes, the lack of an apostrophe has been noted by many.) This, in fact, was once the home of Mary Ann Starkweather and the beginning of the Ypsilanti District Library.

This stately two-story building, with its back facing the picturesque Huron River, was constructed in 1858 for Edwin Mills, a local merchant. Mrs. Starkweather (as she was usually called) and her husband, John, later took ownership after relocating from their farm, where they had lived for about thirty years. The farm allegedly employed Elijah McCoy (of "the Real McCoy" fame) and was said to have been a stop on the Underground Railroad, with McCoy's father, George, serving as conductor. (Eastern Michigan University now sits where the Starkweather farm and award-winning apple orchards once were.)

Both Starkweathers were incredibly generous, giving often to help the village of Ypsilanti grow into the city it is today. (It likely helped that

The Ladies Library, circa 1909. *Ypsilanti Historical Society*.

they had no children to leave their wealth to.) After John's death in 1883, Mrs. Starkweather continued in this vein, eventually donating her house on Huron Street to be the new home of the Ladies Library, the first of the library's locations to be both a standalone building and entirely owned by it.

It seems, however, that Mrs. Starkweather may not have left her home, or at least comes to visit when she can. Radio station WFMK wrote on its website, "Then some 'genius' decided to turn the old house into an office building. According to locals and nearby EMU students, this change of operations did not go over well with Mary Starkweather's spirit." She is said to be the one responsible for the disembodied footsteps employees have heard walking the second floor of the building. One janitor claims to have been touched by her in the basement. Starkweather's apparition has also been seen on the second floor, and guests to the building have heard voices of people who were not there. The Ladies Library is now privately owned, and it's a mystery whether or not Mrs. Starkweather still makes her presence known to those visiting.

The Michigan Avenue Branch

What is now the downtown branch of the Ypsilanti District Library located on Michigan Avenue, where it intersects with Adams Street, initially opened its doors in 1915 as the Carnegie Post Office. The post office moved out in 1962, relocating just around the corner to its present location (108 South Adams Street). At about that same time, the Library Association was looking around for a new home for its growing library collection. A petition was circulated in the community that convinced the city government to purchase the old post office building from the federal government for the library's use for a grand total of one dollar.

Initially, the library took up only the main floor of the building. After a few years, the basement was renovated by the Ypsilanti Historical Society and used as the first location of the Ypsilanti Historical Museum. A few years later, it outgrew that location as well and relocated to its present location (220 North Huron Street). The lower level then became the new home of the library's youth department.

Ypsilanti's post office, circa 1950. *Ypsilanti Historical Society.*

The *Haunted Mitten* podcast was invited to join an incredible evening of ghost investigation at the downtown branch of Ypsilanti's public library in June 2023. Kay went to the event, prepared with a notebook and smartphone (including audio recorder and camera for taking what she hoped were a few ghostly photos). The evening began with an introduction by Scott, a former library employee and the then host of the paranormal group that meets there every other month or so. He introduced the investigation leaders of the evening: John, a docent at the Ypsilanti Historical Museum; Mike, a former police officer; and Amy, spook enthusiast for more than thirty years. After a brief explanation of who they were and what kinds of tools would be used for the investigation, three stations were set up in the library.

The first was up in the "Mezzanine," an attic-like space above the main floor composed of metal grate flooring, duct work and a very eerie spiral staircase ascending from basement to Mezzanine. Maintenance staff have experienced an unfriendly and overwhelming male presence there, as well as shadow people darting through the darkness. Mike set up a spirit box (the device that runs through radio frequencies).

The second was the main floor of the library, where John pulled out his pendulum and audio recorder. Think of the pendulum like a talking/spirit board: there is a mat below it, labeled with "yes," "no," the alphabet and numbers. The pendulum is held above the mat, and questions are asked aloud. The pendulum, whether by unconscious hand movements or another entity, swings or rotates, pointing to answers on the mat.

The third area was the basement, used for the youth section, Teen Zone, and program rooms. Amy set up there with dowsing rods and an audio recorder. Dowsing rods have been used for centuries, with a long history of finding water, ore or even escaped prisoners. They are believed by some investigators to sense changing energies and move based on where those energies are converging. Three people had dowsing rods in the Teen Zone area of the basement. Pages have experienced cold spots, footsteps and unseen presences watching them from around bookshelves.

Split into three groups of about five people each, Kay began her investigation in the Mezzanine. The space is spooky on its own, mostly used for storage of ductwork, HVAC and various maintenance materials. Everyone stood around the spirit box and let it run through radio stations a moment before asking questions. Nothing responded to Mike, the host, but there were odd noises seemingly responding to the group when investigators with a more feminine voice asked questions. (This would become a theme

The Teen Zone, where the investigation ramped up. *Kay Gray*.

of the evening as the group moved through the library.) A few garbled responses came through, possibly of an entity no older than seventeen that was reluctant to tell too much personal information. But they were hardly finished with the group after everyone left the Mezzanine.

Down in the Teen Zone, the investigation really heated up. As it turned out, there were three women highly in tune with the spiritual world among the investigators that evening, and they tapped into a very strong presence. While using the dowsing rods was getting some results, the mediums in the group were tapping into the energy of a young woman of seventeen. None of them had been in the attic with the previous group to hear their short conversation with the seventeen-year-old. She was quite shy, childlike, and didn't want to say much without her mother. Over the course of about half an hour to forty-five minutes, the mediums told the group that she had lost her mother at seventeen and passed on herself not very long after in a way that she "didn't like."

The dowsing rods responded to the presence's answers of yes and no, crossing and uncrossing as the group asked the spirit questions about herself and her mother. Alias, a page at the library who was present in Kay's group throughout the investigation, was the focus of the night, having asked the majority of questions in the mezzanine and later getting the spirit's attention as well as praise. The girl-like presence had an affinity for Alias and found comfort in the youth section, especially with them. She was very shy, and the mediums got the impression that she died sometime in the 1890s and wasn't from the area. But she enjoyed the feelings of comfort and safety that the library brought. This would be the other theme of the evening.

Kay's group spoke with her for a while, but the mediums felt her drift away eventually, especially after she was given confirmation that they would be willing to assist her in crossing over if she wanted the help. The activity in the room died down, and nothing was received during a short EVP session except for some very faint, jumbled noise.

Back on the main floor, John and the second group of investigators had success with the pendulum. Together they seemed to contact a man whose last name was Lokum. He was not from the area either but "traveled the rivers" around the United States, if not the world, and had stopped in Ypsilanti for a time. He chose the library for its safe and comfortable nature. He told John and their group of his three sons, what he did for a living and where he was originally from (Scandinavia). Watching John use the pendulum was fascinating, and although nothing was captured on his audio recorder, just getting relevant answers to questions asked was thrilling.

The night ended with a debriefing where everyone compared their experiences. Overall, it was an exciting evening! None of the investigators saw any shadow people, but using the tools provided, and having three mediums present that night, created an entrancing investigation. There are plans to continue the investigation in small snippets over the next few years, creating a "sampling" of what the downtown library may contain regarding the paranormal. Meetings are open to anyone interested in the phenomena—no experience required!

STONE AND SPOON

The retail space located at 110 West Michigan Avenue in downtown Ypsilanti has been many things over the past century or two. According to the Ann Arbor LocalWiki, this "Italianate style commercial building" was constructed in the 1840s. Unfortunately, the oldest business listed at this location at the Ypsilanti Historical Society is M&E Simpson Millery, which operated here from 1916 to 1931. From 1932 to 1941, it was Hardy's Millinery. Moray's Jewelry called 110 home from 1942 to 1995 and was joined by Max G. Stoakes Optometrist in 1947. A women's clothing store called Mirror's operated here from 1996 to 2006. After this, it was Look in the Attic, an antique home hardware business that now operates exclusively online.

Stone and Spoon, as well as the now online-only Unicorn Feed and Supply. *Kay Gray*.

Jen Eastridge, who also owns Unicorn Feed and Supply (which moved from a brick-and-mortar store to online only at the beginning of 2024), opened Stone and Spoon at 110 in early 2020. Like a lot of downtown Ypsilanti's stores, Stone and Spoon has a deep basement constructed of the relics of Ypsi's past. Like its name suggests, the store carries kitchen essentials and luxury items, as well as unique soaps, teas and goods crafted by local Michigan artists. But it is also home to something, or someone, else. The employees have named her Annabelle.

"We've had three people come in," said Jen, "who have never experienced anything quite like that." "That" being a spirit affectionately named Annabelle. The first person to feel the strong feminine presence was a woman who came to interview Jen before Stone and Spoon was open. They were talking in Unicorn Feed and Supply during the early days of the COVID-19 pandemic when an employee needed to make a video call maskless. Needing a place to continue the interview, Jen suggested they go take a look at the just-leased space for Stone and Spoon.

While in the basement, the interviewer was overcome with emotion immediately. "As soon as we got down the steps, she was making a bee

The basement of Stone and Spoon, where Annabelle has been felt. *Kay Gray*.

line up to the front right there, and up on that little area," Jen said. "She knelt on the floor, and she started weeping. She was just kind of dumbstruck. And she was like, 'I've never felt anything like this before.'" She gathered herself after the intense experience, and they finished their interview away from the basement.

"That little area" is a small section of raised flooring, near the front of the store's basement. The wall behind it is original stonework, complete with old windows still with panes intact. Unremarkable at first glance, the spot has been noted by two others who have visited the store's basement.

A friend of Jen's, who says she is sensitive to spirits, was able to offer a little more information on whoever is still hanging around the store. She felt that the presence in this particular area was feminine, probably young. But perhaps the most surprising bit of information was that the spirit may have been pregnant when she passed, *if* she was a living human who passed on.

And an employee of another Ypsilanti shop had an experience of her own in the exact same spot. While Jen said she couldn't go to the basement with her, she gave the employee permission to check it out. Jen told us, "She [the employee] said that [the spirit] did not feel like she wanted her here. But she was a child. She said that when she would think she'd see [the spirit], and she'd look, it was like she'd hide behind something. She said that behavior is kind of young. She could tell as she was making her way out that she was right there behind her. It was a very polite get out."

Annabelle, Jen said, does not feel malicious. In fact, the staff say hello and goodbye to her often as they come and go through the store. "I've always felt a really warm, loving energy in this space from the moment I walked in, and it's always felt very female-centric to me, like very much a feminine energy." She added, "As long as we can coexist amicably, we are really cool with her being here."

A few other things have happened on the main floor of the store, including a very sturdy candle moving on its own several times. Cody, the assistant manager, set a heavy, solid candle on top of a flat surface near the back of the shop. She left, only to return to find the candle on the floor, several feet away, upright. She put the candle back, only to have the exact same thing happen again. No one else was in the store with Cody, and the candle did not look as if it had been knocked over or fell on its own. It was upright both times it ended up on the floor.

Overall, Stone and Spoon is an open, welcoming space, to those living and not, and it is an essential part of Ypsilanti. The store carries everything a kitchen might need. For the living, that is.

GO! ICE CREAM

I scream, you scream, we all scream for…ghosts? Go! Ice Cream was a popular destination located in the heart of downtown Ypsilanti. Its unique and interesting flavors were made in house from scratch and often included locally sourced ingredients like Michigan-grown strawberries and milk products from nearby dairy farms. Sadly, Go! Ice Cream closed its doors in late 2023.

Like much of the rest of downtown Ypsilanti, the building that housed the ice creamery and attached parlor is more than one hundred years old. More is known about the history of the older rear building. According to Go's owner, Rob Hess, the back part of what is now two buildings mushed together into one first appeared on insurance maps in 1907. It was labeled as a wine bar. Prior to Go! moving in, it was home to an insurance office. When Go! took control of the property, it had to be gutted and built back up to suit the needs of an ice creamery. The process revealed many of the original wine bar decorations, such as leaves painted on the walls.

He guessed that the front part of the building that faces Washington Street, where the party room and other businesses were located, was constructed in the 1920s or '30s. By 1987, the front building had become home to Solway Vision Care. It has also housed a gym and a hair salon.

The basement of the rear building is a real puzzle. A surprisingly well-crafted staircase with polished wood rail leads to a maze of rooms that were perhaps once used as offices. For an old basement, the woodwork is surprisingly fine. There is also a very secure walk-in safe with thick concrete walls that is now used as a storage closet and a disused restroom. What precisely these rooms (minus the restroom) served as in the past is not known.

Former staff of Go! have stories about the store, but it was not until a few years ago that they started talking with one another about them. Interested in sharing the spookier side of Go!, owner Rob hosted an event all about its ghosts. "I did like a post about the haunted ice cream store around October. And that's when the staff that works here now were like, 'Okay, well, let me tell you what we've got.'"

And boy did they have stories. Two employees were opening the store one day around 11:00 a.m., both in the basement to gather the supplies needed for the day, when they heard the front door bell chime and footsteps. Thinking that somehow the main door was unlocked, they raced up to help the customer only to find no one in the store. Hess said the two are still freaked out by the experience to this day.

The sign for Go! Ice Cream, welcoming customers to the shop. *Kay Gray*.

Footsteps are a common thing to hear at Go!, especially when the store is closed. Hess has heard the unmistakable sound of children scampering around their party room late at night, even though no one but him was in the store. His office in the basement was located directly under that area of the store, and he heard all kinds of noises up above him from both living people and what seemed to be phantoms. He said, "Just recently [January 2023] when the building was closed and locked, no one was coming in because we were on a break. So no employees. There's nobody in the other spaces. I know there's nobody in the building, and I just hear footsteps up here. A lot of times it's little kids' footsteps."

And there may even be someone attached to those footsteps. Two employees were once in the kitchen, which has several windows and a windowed door looking into it, busy crafting their signature flavors. Employees know to keep an eye out through those windows while the shop is open, and movement

The door and window where the little boy was seen. *Kay Gray*.

out of the corner of the store manager's eye caught their attention. Well, when one person looks, everyone looks, so the assistant manager also glanced toward the front room of the store. The manager stepped out of the kitchen to tell the little boy to go up front and that they would be helped shortly. But there was no longer anyone there. Hess is adamant they claim they saw a solid person, not a see-through apparition or a reflection in the glass.

And then, ten days later, Hess and an employee were in the kitchen, right by those same windows, when Hess felt a tug on his apron; the knot came undone, with the strings falling to his sides. Certain that he had tied it, he found it strange but not frightening. The employee who was with him, whom Hess described as "no-nonsense," had a slightly different view of the event. They saw the string of his apron go straight out to the side, taut, and tug the knot undone. "It was freaky," Hess said.

However, it must be said that Hess and his employees were not afraid of whatever or whoever inhabits the building. "I just kind of feel like there's a little kid who haunts here who is a ghost here, and it's not unhappy that the place where they are turned into an ice cream store around them....It never has felt malicious or malevolent. It feels like, you know, just a little bit tricky and [a] playful kind of thing."

It will be interesting to see if any future tenants have similar experiences.

OCCIDENTAL HOTEL AND YPSILANTI SANITARIUM AND MINERAL BATH HOUSE

If you are sad, with sickness worn,
And have the headache every morn,
Just come and drink a healing horn,
Of Ypsilanti's water.
—from "Ypsilanti's Water," by A Farmer

In the late nineteenth and early twentieth centuries, the Occidental Hotel was *the* place to be in Ypsilanti. The Occidental was built alongside the Ypsilanti Sanitarium and Mineral Bath House in 1883. Taking up much of the 10s block on the east side of North Huron Street, both businesses officially opened in January 1884.

Unfortunately, on the evening of April 12, 1893, a devastating tornado struck Ypsilanti, completely wiping out or badly damaging many of the

The entrance to the Occidental Hotel, circa 1907. *Ypsilanti Historical Society.*

businesses downtown, including those along Huron Street. Miraculously, no one died as a result of the dreadful storm, and injuries were minimal. However, the same could not be said for several homes and buildings. According to Russ Jones, co-owner and co-founder of Evenstar's Chalice along with Mara Evenstar, the parking lot located on North Huron Street between Michigan Avenue and Pearl Street is thanks to that tornado. The smashed up buildings were torn down and never replaced. The Occidental Hotel and Sanitarium were rebuilt, updated with the latest technology, and eventually reopened. After all, the healing properties of the local mineral water represented big business along the Huron River, and the hotel and sanitarium owners were not going to let a storm get in the way of business.

It was claimed that drinking Ypsilanti's mineral water could cure anything from rheumatism to cancer. Patients were even said to throw away their crutches after receiving treatment at the Sanitarium. According to a whole-page ad for the Sanitarium in the *Cleary College Journal* from 1899, there were reported to be "3,437 grains of mineral matter" in each gallon of spring water. This amount was considered so potent that even undergoing a bath treatment in the water without the supervision of an experienced doctor was considered dangerous.

Potential patients were advised to first consult with their family physician and obtain a written letter with a diagnosis, which they brought with them to the Sanitarium and handed over to the house physician. (This is how you knew the Sanitarium was genuine—it had its own medical staff.) They were then to undertake the water treatment exactly as prescribed. This may last for a week or possibly two, and healing would continue "for a long time afterwards." Should any operations be required during a person's stay, the Sanitarium was ready for it. "A large operating room, with complete equipment, is kept for the use of physicians, both local and foreign, who may care to bring their patients here to be operated upon." Don't have your own physician handy? No need to worry! "Operations can be performed, if required, by the staff surgeon."

The Sanitarium contained forty bathing rooms for both freshwater and mineral water baths, separate parlors for men and women, a smoking room, a reading room, rooms for mineral vapor and foot baths and a room for dry sweating. Those being treated, and those who had traveled from out of town, could stay at the Occidental Hotel, which also housed a popular

Mineral Bath House and Occidental Hotel, date unknown. *Ypsilanti Historical Society*.

banquet hall. The *Ann Arbor Argus* newspaper reported in April 1891 that the "first annual banquet of The U. of M. Daily was held at the Occidental Hotel in Ypsilanti," which featured representatives from prominent student newspapers as far away as Yale, Harvard, Cornell and Princeton.

Evenstar's Chalice—along with its neighbors Twisted Things Boutique, World of Rocks and others—now makes up the space that once housed the Occidental Hotel and Sanitarium. Jones believes that this trio of businesses were once the hotel's dining room, where meals cost a mere twenty-five cents each. The former hotel rooms upstairs were long ago converted into apartments.

Evenstar's Chalice

Although the space looks very different from when it was a hotel, one can only imagine that the peaceful, rejuvenating feeling permeating the air could be felt across the decades. As its name might hint, Evenstar's Chalice carries what it calls "sacred swag," items one may need to enhance their spiritual practices and spiritual spaces. Singing bowls ring out their pure tones, tarot readings are performed for customers on the regular and beautiful art adorns the tables and walls.

Most of the spirits that visit the store do just that—visit. Beverly Fish—teacher, psychic, channeler and often a reader for Evenstar's Chalice—described the spirits as "anonymous" to her. They don't stop and chat, but rather move through the building as if it were still the Occidental or Sanitarium. She couldn't say if the people had died there, but she also couldn't think of another reason their spirits would still be hanging around.

A notable incident at the store that had nothing to do with the building itself involved a statue carved from wood that Jones thought may have been Polynesian in origin. Mother, as she is called, is made of a dark wood, stands about twenty-four inches tall if not more and has a string of large shells draped around her thin neck. Jones said that it was Mara Evenstar who picked the statue up from a thrift store and brought it in. They put the statue by the front door and asked her to protect the store. Evidently, she took this request too literally. Jones said, "From the time we put her up there to the time we took her down, there wasn't a single customer that came in the store."

This lasted for about two days. The statue was relocated to one of the back rooms and told to protect the back door instead. This is where Beverly

Fish encountered her. Fish said, "I was coming back and I said, 'What's back here?' Because I remember when I got past a certain place, it felt really…like you're pushing against all the bad energy."

The decision was made that the statue had to go. Being the expert on these matters, Fish took Mother. She explained, "I wrapped her up and I sealed her up and put her in my car and drove up [to Sault Ste. Marie]." She told the statue, "I'm going to take you to some people who really love you," and asked her to not do "anything to me in the car while driving." It's a long drop from the Mackinac Bridge to the Straits below!

After arriving in Sault Ste. Marie, Fish met Greg and Dana Newkirk, owners and operators of the Newkirk Museum of the Paranormal and hosts of the *Haunted Objects* podcast, who were in town for the annual Michigan Paranormal Convention. Fish felt certain that Mother would find a good home with the Newkirks, and she was right.

Mother was featured on the podcast in the episode "We've Been Cursed! Deadly Hexes, Witchcraft, and Mormon Bigfoot." The Newkirks relayed the story but said that they "did not get a bad vibe" from her and liked her. She has since joined their collection, and as far as they have said, nothing negative happens around them.

Ben Goldman, creator and director of Afterlife Road Productions, investigated Evenstar's Chalice with his team in 2023 and documented it in a short film. In their investigation, they captured a feminine voice on their spirit box saying "hello" to them. Goldman and another investigator, Michael, witnessed what Goldman described as a "flowy" dress. "I'm looking down the hallway, and I see what looks like just a flowy dress," he said. The two acknowledged silently what the other saw. The moment they had the chance, Goldman continued, "We both darted down to that hallway. And there's papers, flyers of upcoming events, you know, on the wall right there. And they're kind of swaying, like something did just brush by." Michael asked the spirit box, "Was that you we just saw?" And the spirit box, in the same feminine voice said, "Thank you, Michael."

The team also captured an unusually hot antique cross on their thermal camera. They experimented with different surfaces and reflections, trying to find out if it was the glass the cross sat behind causing the odd high temperature reading, but they found nothing conclusively explaining why the item was significantly warmer than the rest of the room. Ben did concede that the anomaly could have been caused by the glass reflecting heat back, but it was still an odd thing to happen during the investigation.

Twisted Things

A local artist's co-op haven, Twisted Things is a unique space. The front half of the store carries everything from handmade mosquito spray to crafted dice to stickers and patches. The back half of the store, however, shows off its spookier side. Candles, herbs for spellcraft and even Ouija boards made from wooden church doors (crafted by the relative of the man who made the doors, in fact) can be found in the low-lit, moody room. The one-of-a-kind items all have a story.

But something else can be found in the walls of Twisted Things as well. The store is especially active at the end of the day after closing, making it uncomfortable for employees to stay late. Disembodied footsteps have been heard coming right up to the counter, as if someone is waiting in line or impatient for employees to leave. There is a rumor of a ghost cat hanging around the shop, but this could not be verified.

Russ Jones and Beverly Fish of Evenstar's Chalice postulated that because this block was once all united as the Occidental Hotel and Ypsilanti Sanitarium, the spirits that are observed in today's individual stores travel between them, ignoring the walls that did not exist back in their day.

The modern view of Huron Street, now divided into shops and apartments. *Kay Gray.*

Whether spirits linger from the long-gone Sanitarium and hotel or not, Twisted Things is a unique space with myriad stories from the artists who sell their wares.

World of Rocks

With its tables filled with rocks and stones gathered from all over the globe, World of Rocks is an exciting destination in downtown Ypsilanti. Whether you are an amateur geologist, a jeweler who works with stones, a believer in the healing power of crystals or just curious about the countless minerals that make up our planet, World of Rocks is a must-stop that has been a part of the Ypsi community for more than two decades.

In the days of the Occidental Hotel and Ypsilanti Sanitarium, there were stairways on the exteriors of the buildings allowing patrons to access the basement facilities without going through the interior of the buildings. Nowadays, those stairways have been covered up by sidewalks, but in the basement of World of Rocks, the original storefront still exists and can be seen by those lucky few who are allowed access. And indeed, the original façade of that part of the building is there, complete with windows and what could possibly be the original flooring. It looks as if it could be dug out from the street, dusted off and used to light the basement once again!

However, employees tend to stay away from this area of the basement, as well as the spare bathroom that is just around the corner. One employee said that the basement gave off creepy feelings, and no one really liked being down there for any length of time. There is something oddly unsettling about it, from the submerged original walls to the lone bathroom to the unfinished look of things, as if renovations were stopped halfway through completion. Some of the outer walls even have chiseled initials in them, but their owners are unknown. Whatever is going on down there, the weird experiences don't stop once employees reach the top of the stairs.

"Tumbled stones will stop and fall just right out," one employee said, referencing the bowls of polished stones in baskets and containers all over the store. "Nobody will get hurt, nothing will ever break." But stones will hop out of their bowls or fall off of flat shelves and onto the floor regularly. Poster putty has become the standard adhesive of choice when displaying larger items because of how frequently they like to end up on the wood floors or even in another display across the store. Some employees "tell the rocks goodnight every night" in order to keep whatever mischief could be caused at bay.

YPSILANTI OPERA HOUSE

Little is known about the original Ypsilanti Opera House other than it was a beloved part of Ypsilanti and featured numerous prominent shows as well as speakers. It was all but entirely destroyed in the infamous 1893 tornado (newspapers at the time called it a cyclone) that laid waste to much of the downtown area. The storm hit on April 12 at around 7:00 p.m. when many were finishing up their dinners. Despite the extensive damage, no one perished.

The Opera House, empty at the time, collapsed, with only its front wall remaining upright. Debris from the Opera House damaged the next-door hotel, the Hawkins House, where upper floors of the hotel fell onto the floors below, taking guests with them.

The second Opera House was built on the same site at the end of the nineteenth century, and you can still see its original front along Michigan Avenue. According to an *Ann Arbor Democrat* article from September 17, 1897, that reported a change in management, "Ypsilanti has a large class

Opposite: The Ypsilanti Opera House before the cyclone. *Ypsilanti Historical Society.*

Above: Damage done to downtown Ypsilanti just after the cyclone. *Ypsilanti Historical Society.*

of theater lovers and an untiring endeavor will be made to satisfy the most exacting desires of this portion of the community." There was clearly a lot to live up to.

In the early part of the twentieth century, the Opera House began showing moving pictures. In 1920, the Opera House was operating as the Wuerth Theater, which it remained until closing in 1959. Then as now, shops and other businesses flanked the entrance to the theater. As of 2023, the lobby remained but had been converted into retail space. The auditorium was torn down in 1959 to expand parking options in the rear of the building on North Adams Street.

What was once part of the building that held the Opera House are Star Studio, an empty retail space (as of 2024), and the Conjure Goddess, a metaphysical retail store with a specialty in African-based religions and faiths that sadly closed its brick-and-mortar doors in early 2024 and moved to online only. In 1959, this space was a restaurant.

As you might expect, a host of activity was reported in such a spiritual store. Doors had a habit of opening and closing on their own, and items fell off very sturdy shelves. But what you might not expect when you're in the bright, welcoming space during the daylight is that there was a masculine presence that did not like anyone staying in the store past 11:00 p.m. or 12:00 p.m. And he made that very known. Activity increased and employees felt uncomfortable, as if someone were willing them to leave.

Employees had heard that there had once been a bad fire in the building when it was still the Opera House, and they speculated that perhaps someone had died, resulting in the male presence. No newspaper reports could be found to verify this. However, there's no telling what manner of spirits may be lurking at the site of the old Opera House. But this is far from the only disgruntled basement entity in Ypsilanti that doesn't like when employees work overtime.

Holly Bones, local artist and force behind the annual Holy Bones festival and other events, used to run a gallery and gift shop called Stardust located in the former lobby. When asked if she had any experiences while she was there, she quipped, "All of the strange happenings I experienced were caused by the living." Touché.

RIVERSIDE ARTS CENTER

What is now the Riverside Arts Center (RAC) was once two separate buildings in downtown Ypsilanti. The larger side on the north end was once a Masonic temple built in 1909. The basement, presumably where the North Gallery is now, once housed a bowling alley for the community's entertainment. There were also multiple parlors, for men and for women, as well as a billiard room, an auditorium, a kitchen and a dining room with seating up to four hundred. The third and fourth floors were where the Masonic rites were performed and members initiated. This building was the first in Washtenaw County to be built specifically for Masonic use. The Masons remained at this location until 1987, when they moved to a new location (with more parking) in Ypsilanti Township, and the building was sold to the now closed antique store Materials Unlimited, which used it for storage.

The Off Center Gallery, the southern building that makes up the RAC, was once the Detroit Energy (DTE) Building and was built in 1915. This is where locals would go to pay their energy bills in the days before online payments became the norm. Although its offices were closed in the 1990s, DTE still maintains electrical conduits in the basement and a transformer

The groundbreaking ceremony for the Masonic Temple on Huron Street. *Ypsilanti Historical Society.*

farm in the back, and the RAC rents the building from DTE for one dollar per year.

The alley that once ran between the two buildings has been covered over and walled in (it is known as the garage), and an elevator was added to make each floor of the RAC accessible.

While still serving as the Masonic Temple, on November 29, 1924, the building was badly damaged by a fire that raged for four hours before it could be extinguished. After extensive repairs, it was rededicated the following June. The upper floors were damaged by a second fire in 1970. The RAC was able to recently renovate the top floor into a beautiful rentable space that contains a kitchenette, bathroom and fireplace.

The hosts of *Haunted Mitten* had the distinct privilege of being the first ghost investigators to be able to come into Riverside. A team went in knowing a few of the experiences people have had within the building. Marisa Dluge and Greg Pizzino, members of the Neighborhood Theatre Group (NTG), have both seen shadow people within the garage area of Riverside. Dluge

Some of the equipment used for the investigation of the Riverside Arts Center. *Kay Gray*.

used to manage the Center, and she has had multiple experiences with the shadow person and has heard strange voices and noises, both during busy rehearsals and quiet days alone. Pizzino saw a shadow person during rehearsals for NTG's *Black Cat: A New Nightmare* in the fall of 2023.

Haunted Mitten's investigation took place less than a week after Black Cat's closing performance. Crysta, Kay and Greg were joined by employees from Riverside, making nine people in total investigating. Armed with an infrared camera, EMF (electromagnetic field) meter, flashlights, thermometers, audio recorders and a plethora of smartphones, they explored the four-story linked buildings over the course of two hours.

Everyday, normal-looking buildings can get spooky in the dark. But add in a huge, dusty basement and several darkened stairways and even the most benign of buildings can look sinister. The team went top to bottom, beginning in the newly renovated top floor. The EMF meter jumped around wildly there, reading as high as 13.0, when the rest of the building was solidly below 1.0. It's thought that ghosts can manipulate electromagnetic fields, using them to gain energy to manifest in physical ways. And while they didn't see or hear anything on that floor with their own ears, a strange drip was caught on Kay's recorder, like water dripping from a faucet. There is a faucet on that floor, but one of the investigators confirmed that it was not running.

Most of the floors were quiet, the spirits serene, possibly unwilling to come out to communicate with the staff of the RAC. Other than the strange dripping sound that was picked up on Kay's phone recorder, and was not heard by anyone in person, or on Greg's phone recording when reviewed later, they received nothing else until they reached the basement. There are several smaller rooms branching off the main room at the bottom of the stairs that lead to other storage areas, some of which are used by DTE (including a small room with a very dangerous conduit that everyone was warned not to go near). On the opposite side of the large basement from that room, Greg ventured into a small, mostly empty side chamber, his phone still recording. "Entering the empty side room with the pillars," he said, "I distinctly heard the sound of fabric brushing up against the concrete wall. Checking with my flashlight, I looked for any indication of a possible rodent that may have made the noise.…The room was completely empty. I next tried to replicate the sound, walking in and out of the room, making sure my bag brushed against the doorway in case I had somehow made the sound myself but could not duplicate it."

Kay was doing an EVP session at the time, and these sounds happened while the group asked questions. One particular question got a response. When asked if whoever was down there would like people to ask permission before doing remodeling in the building, there was a tap from somewhere in the room. When asked if the spirit would like the group to leave the basement, another loud noise was heard, not just over the recorder, but by the group in person. Taking that as the signal to leave, Kay instructed everyone to head back upstairs.

There, Greg was the subject of another interaction. "While Kay was collecting the group, something made physical contact, jabbing me in the side of the head. While the nature of the physical contact did not feel aggressive, it did feel as if someone was showing me who was boss in the space, which lined up with the responses Kay received in the basement when she asked whether the spirits there wanted people to ask permission before working in that area."

While no apparitions appeared, the noises heard over audio and Greg's physical interaction with something are very interesting to say the least. Combined with past and current managers' experiences, Riverside Arts Center may indeed have some Masons or other folks wandering around that may call the connected buildings home.

YPSILANTI HISTORICAL SOCIETY

While it may not be the oldest house in Ypsilanti, the current location of the Ypsilanti Historical Society (YHS) museum and archives was and is certainly one of the most important. It was built in 1860 by Asa and Minerva Dow (no relation to Herbert Henry Dow, founder of Dow Chemical). Asa Dow was the president of the First National Bank of Ypsilanti and one of the founders of the Ypsilanti Woolen Mills, two companies that helped Ypsi thrive in the early days. Both he and another familiar name to locals, Daniel L. Quirk, founded these companies. Unfortunately, Dow's wife, Minerva, would not get to enjoy her home for long. She died in 1864, at the age of thirty-seven. Shortly after her death, Dow moved back to Chicago, where he had lived prior to moving to Ypsilanti. After his death, his body was laid to rest beside Minerva's at Ypsilanti's Highland Cemetery.

The Goodrich family bought the house from Dow, and Aaron Goodrich took over management of the Follett House in Depot Town. They shared the home with servants and boarders and stayed until 1879. They passed the house to Lambert Barnes and his family. Barnes was and is a huge name in Ypsilanti. Lambert Barnes was president of the Peninsular Paper Company and the mayor twice. His wife, Jane, was the daughter of Robert L. Geddes, another name locals will instantly recognize, and readers of this book will, too, later on. The house was added onto significantly, including a second story built on top of the kitchen at the back of the house, and a wrap-around porch was taken off the side of the house. A carriage house was added to the back as well.

The Barnes children continued living in the house until 1922, when it was sold and turned into apartments. The City of Ypsilanti did not buy the house until 1966. The last tenant did not move out until 1970, however, and it was then that the house was offered to the historical society. Blessedly, the original construction and even stenciling on the walls had been preserved behind façades, and turning the apartments back into a single-family home did not require work as extensive as it could have. The Ypsilanti Historical Society opened its museum in 1972. The archives were not located in the building until the late 2000s.

There have been rumors of a haunting at the historical society for a long time. A lot of historical societies are rumored to be haunted, as they are the collectors of history and artifacts from an area's past, and those things have a habit of leaving a mark on the directors, volunteers and visitors in one way or another. It seems that the Ypsilanti Historical Society may have more than one entity floating through its archives and museum. In fact, its volunteers consider it the most haunted building in the city.

Many moons ago, as one might say, local historian James Mann (whom you might recognize from many of the sources in this book's bibliography) had his own encounter with one of the resident ghosts. He heard a woman singing while in the archives in the basement one evening, and while he did not admit that it was a ghost, he related that it might have been Minerva Dow. She has been seen several times over the years, dressed in gray. She is not relegated to the basement either. According to the *Ann Arbor News*, "Standing behind the Dow Home where the Historical Society used to be housed, [George] Ridenour noticed a lady in the second story of the Dow Home. She appeared 'lonely and forlorn' and Ridenour turned to his friends and told them he had just seen a ghost." He believed that ghost to be Mrs. Dow. While on a later search for "the Gray Lady," Ridenour smelled perfume in not only one room of the historical society but also on both the first and second floors. One friend with him smelled it as well; the other did not.

George had another encounter with Minerva on his second visit to the property. He was in the sunroom, enjoying a beautiful autumn day, when he had a strange encounter. "I wondered if Minerva, herself, had stood here and enjoyed the view. It was then that I became aware of a whiff of perfume. I looked around and found no plants in bloom, no flowers, no one cleaning." He went upstairs to the second floor and again smelled the perfume. "In two of the rooms, I again smelled the distinct scent of perfume. Again, I was ALONE. While not filling me with fear I was relieved at the clomping of shoes on the hardwood floor." He was joined by his companions, who at first did not smell anything, but the docent exclaimed, "Wait, I smell it too. Strong odor of perfume." The three decided to leave Minerva be and head back to the first floor, but George referred to it thereafter as the "scent of Minerva."

A volunteer for the historical society has also had strange encounters while in the building. Lights have a habit of turning themselves on, and this has been experienced by more than volunteer. One person Kay spoke to said, "We were having a late-night class in the archives basement and the museum was completely closed and dark from the first floor up. The class wanted to order pizza, so when it got here I went upstairs in what was a completely dark house to go to the front door. I turned on the hallway light to get the pizza from the delivery boy. When I turned around and turned off the hallway light every single light on the second floor was on."

The Ypsilanti Historical Society in 2023. *Kay Gray.*

Much like for a fair number of businesses in Ypsilanti, when the sun starts setting, uneasy feelings start emerging here. As volunteers close up the building each night, they are followed by a presence that gives them the distinct feeling of being ushered out quickly. They refer to these presences as "the night crew" that comes in when the living beings leave for the day. And the head of that crew has a very distinct personality. "Researchers in the past have also interacted with a little boy who we at YHS call George (aka King George) because he likes to think he runs the joint. There was an intern several years ago who was in the basement before it was the archives....When she turned around to go upstairs, she saw a little boy with red eyes grinning at her in the doorway. She was horrified and inconsolable for some time. If Georgie boy wants you to see him, you'll see him," the volunteer said.

Current volunteers are not sure that George is a little boy at all, but rather something more malicious. However, he has yet to show his true colors to any staff or guests. A volunteer expressed their thoughts that something sinister may lurk in the attic as well. These two entities could be connected, or they could be the same spirit that thinks it owns the historical society for one reason or another. A Facebook post by the historical society from October 2020 states, "Most of us do not believe in ghosts, but we all prefer not to be in the house alone at night." With so many of Ypsilanti's artifacts, documents and history contained within one building's walls, it is no surprise that staff and guests alike often experience strange phenomena. And perhaps Minerva Dow continues to enjoy the home she never got to truly know, watching over the preservation of not only her history but also that of the entire city.

INTERLUDE

A HISTORY OF YPSILANTI THROUGH ITS CEMETERIES

Ypsilanti's motto should really be: "Wherever you are, you are standing on a grave." Before beginning this book, the authors knew of three cemeteries in the general Ypsilanti region: Highland, St. John the Baptist and Soop. They had already been to Soop to check out its spooky reputation. St. John's is the Catholic cemetery on River Street, and Highland is the large, beautiful cemetery across the street from it. It's a great place to walk a dog or just hang out and enjoy the beautiful landscape.

But what most of Ypsi's residents probably don't know is that they are never far from a burial ground, no matter where in the city or township they are. Ypsilanti, long ago, was a major trail for the local Native American communities, namely, the Ojibwe, Potawatomi and Odawa (otherwise known collectively as the Anishinaabe). But plenty of other people made use of the trail that is now essentially Michigan Avenue. There is even evidence of burial mounds in the area, although unfortunately some of them have been excavated without permission or even archaeological intent. It is thought that there was at least one where Highland Cemetery sits now. There may have also been a small village of Indigenous people, perhaps permanent, perhaps temporary, somewhere in the northeastern part of Ypsilanti proper.

WEST CEMETERY

The earliest cemetery belonging to Ypsilanti itself (then known as Ypsilanti Village) was located at what is now the intersection of Michigan Avenue and Summit Street, where a rental house and Avenue Market, a party store, now sit. According to Charles Chapman in his 1881 book *History of Washtenaw County*, as quoted in *Ypsilanti Gleanings*, "West Cemetery was the first cemetery for the village of Ypsilanti. It was a rude burial place and was used from 1830–1847 and was to be the resting place for between 150–250 persons." It has also been known as First Cemetery and Summit Cemetery, both of which are apt names. But it was a matter of contention from the start. The battle over whether bodies should be moved to a more suitable place took several years to resolve, beginning sometime around 1858, through Highland Cemetery's dedication, and wasn't fully decided until 1871. People were outraged at "those even suggesting such a sacrilege."

But vacated West Cemetery was, at least once Highland opened its gates to accept the bodies. In fact, folks had thirty days to move their loved ones to Highland, or the village of Ypsi would do it for them! *Ypsilanti Gleanings* noted that the village vacated the cemetery of every body and moved them to the brand-spankin'-new Highland Cemetery by 1871 "by one man, one horse, one shovel, and one body at a time." The register for West Cemetery has not been found (yet), so unfortunately it is impossible to know how many were buried there before vacancy, as the records modern scholars have to go on were collected after the bodies were relocated to Highland.

According to the Ypsilanti Historical Society, it is very, very likely that not all of the bodies were actually moved. In fact, there are numerous stories of children bringing home human bones that they found in the area of the former cemetery. Their parents, of course, were less than thrilled and demanded that the bones be put right back where they had found them.

In 2016, Michigan playwright Joseph Zettelmaier set out to craft a play about real-life paranormal experiences with contributions from people located all over Michigan's two peninsulas. Three years later, Roustabout Theatre Troupe (of which Zettelmaier was a founding member) produced the result, *Haunted: The Great Lakes Ghost Project*. For three weekends in October 2019, audiences who came to Ypsilanti Experimental Space, located at 8 North Washington Street, were treated to an array of spooky tales each connected by the narrator character, Joe, and anchored by one particular paranormal

The small marker denoting the location of Cross Cemetery. *Kay Gray*.

experience teased throughout the performance and finally revealed at the end. (Spoilers for the play ahead.)

With growing anxiety, Joe relays to the audience his own encounter with the unexplained while attending nearby Eastern Michigan University and living in a house located near the corner of Summit and Michigan. A dark, disturbing figure stood in Joe's room at night. He later learned of the former cemetery on which his apartment may well have been built. Of course, the audience was led to speculate on whether or not the mysterious figure was the spirit of one of the disturbed occupants—its skeleton, perhaps—still buried in the home's yard.

Avenue Market has a 4.3 out of 5 star rating on Google and still looks fresh and bright from a semi-recent remodel. One would never guess by its looks that it was built on top of an old cemetery. But the bottles on the shelves may not be the only spirits sticking around. Although a valuable resource and popular stop for local neighborhood residents, some report feeling strange sensations within, as if there is something just a little off about the store. One frequent customer said that he was not surprised by the cemetery revelation based on his experiences.

Unfortunately, the long perished of Ypsi's first cemetery are not the only deaths associated with Avenue Market. On the afternoon of May 6, 2019, a fight broke out in front of the store, and a sixteen-year-old boy was shot multiple times. A nearby school was locked down out of caution while the shooter was sought by police, and the victim was rushed to the hospital in critical condition. Sadly, he didn't make it. It is unknown with absolute certainty if anything paranormal happens in the area, but with a past like this, one can only guess!

CROSS CEMETERY

At around the same time that First Cemetery was in use, in the 1830s and 1840s, two other graveyards were donated to the good folks of Ypsilanti. Pettibone/Cross Cemetery is now just a small expanse of plants and broken and buried headstones across the street from Highland and St. John the Baptist. The land was originally donated by the Pettibone family in 1830 to the brand-new Superior Township. In fact, several members of the Pettibone family were buried there. But over the years it fell into disrepair, and it was not used for very long. Now it is a sliver of land looking on the much more active and well-cared-for cemeteries across the street. There has been disagreement between those who wish to care for the old graveyard and Superior Township, which seems content to let it be overgrown, tangled and lost. There is now, at least, a small marker on the hill denoting where the cemetery is. A few headstones can still be seen when there isn't snow on the ground. However, there is no parking nearby except for a lot that belongs to a line of apartments. Travel at your own risk.

SPENCER CEMETERY

Spencer Cemetery is located on the corner of Michigan Avenue and Spencer Lane in Ypsilanti Township. The cemetery was used for roughly ninety-two years, from 1833 to 1925. Strong Tower Ministries now occupies the buildings next door, but there is a commemorative plaque where the cemetery "used to" be. About 118 bodies are still buried there. When the Willow Run Community School District, which had been steadily expanding with the growing town since its inception in 1834, needed to widen yet again, it was determined that Spencer Cemetery would be a good place for the playground. The school district had owned the land since 1849, so it was no problem to reallocate the cemetery land. It did away with all the headstones…and left the graves intact. The marker remains along with the residents. However, up until about the mid-1990s, no one would have known that there was anything there except a tangle of brush and a few trees. The marker was so badly grown over that it was no longer visible. Thankfully, the grass has been mowed, and the plaque has been taken care of since then, although it's still easy to miss as you speed down Michigan Avenue.

UNION-UDELL CEMETERY

Union-Udell has a humorous name but a not-so-humorous haunting. It sits off Textile Road just southwest of Willow Run Airport. It butts right up against a mobile home park—they share a fence, in fact. Just under one hundred acres of land were purchased from Lionel Udell in 1845. It was operated by the Union Cemetery Association, hence the combination in the name.

One of the most significant events in the cemetery's history came in February 1992. Vandals struck the sleepy cemetery, damaging twenty grave sites, including the late husband and daughter of one Alice Webb from Belleville. She told the *Ypsilanti Press*, "The loss of them was enough, but to see their graves treated this way hurts." Vandalism had happened occasionally before 1992, but not to that extent. Thankfully, that much destruction has not been documented since.

There is said to be a witch named Elizabeth who haunts Union-Udell. No one knows her backstory, whether she died painfully or peacefully or why she haunts the cemetery at all. Rumor claims that she was a practitioner of witchcraft, but how that leads to haunting a cemetery is not clear. With a minimum of five people named Elizabeth buried in Union-Udell, who is to say which is the witch? However, people have had strange experiences in the cemetery just the same. Shadow figures have been seen darting between graves and trees, always at a distance from the viewer. Primal growling and snarling have been heard in the dark, and investigators have caught things that they can't explain in photos and on video.

SOOP CEMETERY

There is another cemetery close by Union-Udell that is also claimed to have a witch named Elizabeth. Soop Cemetery, formerly known as Pleasantview, was donated for community use by the Soop family in 1832. It is located on the border of Ypsilanti and Van Buren Townships, just off Old Denton Road (not to be confused with Denton Road, where the haunted bridge is, located a ten-minute drive north). Elizabeth lived from 1826 to 1899. Her death certificate said that she died of dropsy, which is an old term for edema, an abnormal accumulation of fluid in the body. How she became the witch of Soop Cemetery is a mystery. The rumor is that she practiced witchcraft, much like the witch of Union-Udell, and that symbols on her grave signify her evil doings. However, the symbols on her grave, a cross through a crown and a ring of roses, do not symbolize anything negative. In fact, they reinforce her belief in the Christian God, as well as signify her purity and beauty.

Elizabeth, the "witch" of Soop Cemetery. *Kay Gray*.

Regardless, the rumor persists that there is a witch haunting Soop Cemetery, with plenty of strange experiences to warrant thrill-seekers and investigators visiting often, including *Haunted Mitten*. While these two investigators didn't personally experience something weird on their visit, other paranormal investigation groups have conducted more thorough searches of the cemetery and have posted their findings to the internet.

Great Lakes Ghost Hunters of Michigan visited in 2018 and caught some EVPs, with one saying "I am here" and another asking, "Whatcha doing?" Neither of these was heard by the team until they later reviewed their audio recorders. A strange mist was captured on video in the middle of the day. Both of these phenomena have been reported as common within Soop Cemetery.

Mysterious Michigan, a website curated by paranormal author Amberrose Hammond, has a collection of stories from commenters about their experiences within Soop. People have seen three- to four-foot-tall shadow figures walking toward them. They have heard footsteps walking beside them when no one else was around. Disembodied voices have shouted at explorers as well as whispered right next to them. Colorful orbs of light have been seen floating through the cemetery after dark as well.

PROSPECT CEMETERY

Although the inscription on the historical marker in Prospect Park labels it the second cemetery in Ypsilanti, by the time of its founding in 1842, Ypsi had been home to several of them. Prospect does have the honor of being Ypsilanti's first public park, however. At the height of its use, Prospect Cemetery had 250 residents interred there, but alas, it was not to last forever. Once Highland Cemetery was up and running, use of Prospect declined sharply.

By 1890, Prospect was a ghost town (pun intended). A group of young women, titling themselves the Park Improvement Society, took it upon themselves to make a change. The historical plaque at the corner of the park reads, "Inspired by a nationwide parks movement, in 1891 a group of local women began working to convert the by-then-neglected cemetery into the city's first park." They raised more than $1,000 to turn Prospect Cemetery into a public park, taking the next few years to move the bodies to Highland Cemetery for reburial. Of course, rumors abound that not all of them were moved. According to legend, when the City of Ypsilanti declared that bodies should be moved out of Prospect Cemetery, it neglected to provide funds or assistance or even a deadline as to when the bodies needed to be out. At least fourteen graves were left behind, and because of lax burial records, not all of the residents could be accounted for.

These days, Prospect Park serves as the playground for Ypsilanti International Elementary School as well as a public park. There are stories of children still finding gravestones on the property, lending to the rumor that not everyone was moved as they should have been. On the grounds is also a cannon, put there in 1902 by former mayor Oliver E. Thompson (also the owner of the Thompson Block in Depot Town). According to Doris Milliman, a local historian from earlier days, "Mayor Thompson found it [at Fort McClary] in 1900 and on hearing it was to be replaced by a large gun, he applied for it. It took two years of correspondence, because of government red tape, to get it assigned to Ypsilanti." And in Prospect it has stood ever since.

KELLY-GRAVES CEMETERY

There will be a brief detour now to Ypsilanti Township, where, behind a grove of lilac trees, sits a very small burial place for a very small community. Comstock Cemetery, also known as the Kelly-Graves Cemetery, is on private property on land between Whittaker, Merritt and Textile Roads. In this little cemetery resides members of the Graves, Kelly, Comstock and Reynolds families. It was used from the 1840s to the 1870s, and there are very few graves there. As it has always been private property, there is little else known about the grounds. But perhaps the homes now surrounding it have their own stories to tell!

HIGHLAND CEMETERY

And thus, we finally reach Highland Cemetery. By its founding in 1864, the city of Ypsilanti was booming. The community needed a much larger place to bury its dead, and in the late 1850s, a board of nine directors comprising prominent men gathered the funds to buy the original forty acres of beautiful forest and farmland at what is now a decent portion of River Street. A few of the men in the association had names found elsewhere in this book: B. Follett and D.L. Quirk. The design was done in the garden-style fashion of the time, with rolling hills and plenty of shade for picnicking, using the natural landscape of the forty acres as inspiration. Historian Al Rudisill wrote of its design, "If you look at an aerial view of the original layout of Highland Cemetery you can see a number of distinct figures designed into the winding roads and paths. The figures include an Eastern Star, a Maltese Cross, a Horseshoe, an Elf Shoe, a Cloverleaf, and a Star of David. The reason for, and the meaning of, these figures remains a mystery." The Maltese Cross specifically has been theorized to represent some secret society. Interestingly, no other cemeteries designed by Colonel James L. Glen, the architect of Highland, contain symbols like these. It is anyone's guess why Highland does.

Just beyond the locally made wrought-iron gates donated to Highland in 1880 is the Starkweather Chapel. It was commissioned by Mary Ann Starkweather in honor of her late husband, John. Starkweather, who inherited money from a deceased uncle and had no children to leave her own fortune to, also presented the Civil War Memorial that resides in the cemetery. Her name is almost everywhere one looks in Ypsilanti, and she was one the biggest contributors to the Ypsilanti that residents know today. She and her husband are both buried at Highland. Other locally notable names to be found on the headstones are Minerva Dow, wife of Asa Dow and the second person to be buried in the cemetery; P. Roger Cleary, founder of Cleary College; and the first person to be buried at Highland, Elias Norton, an early pioneer of the area.

There have been many, many paranormal investigations of Highland Cemetery. During one conducted by a team called the South Lyon Area Paranormal Society (SLAPS) in 2009, the team heard odd noises from time to time, but it wasn't until late into their search that something big happened. At the back of the cemetery, all but one of the investigators, Gerry, left the car to look around. Not long after the rest of the group had gone up a nearby hill, one of the team, Traci, started to worry about Gerry being by himself. That's when he cried out, "Jenny, the car is moving! The car is moving!"

Jenny, head of the SLAPS team, jumped into action. Gerry was in the second row of seats and unable to reach the pedals. Jenny hopped in and stopped the car, which was indeed rolling forward, despite being in park. But that wasn't the scariest part for Gerry. To quote from the SLAPS blog, "Gerry saw a black cape-like figure with a hood coming from the car's left side, telling Gerry 'You will be Sorry.' And then Gerry said that the car started to move, like it was being pushed."

The team left the cemetery shortly after, despite having only been there for a little over an hour and a half. They had no idea who or what it was Gerry saw, but they were not going to stick around to find out.

ST. JOHN THE BAPTIST CATHOLIC CEMETERY

Across the street from Highland Cemetery lies the subtle, sprawling hills of St. John the Baptist. Quiet and peaceful, it is the resting place of the area's Catholic population, but back when it was founded in 1865, it was in a much different location. These days, that original location is more known for housing the students of Eastern Michigan University. But the original location can still be easily found. Just look for the intersection of St. Johns and Ann Streets. St. John the Baptist Catholic Church noted, "In 1865, the men of the 14th Michigan Volunteer Infantry Regiment donated $500 to the Parish. This was a gift in appreciation for the many acts of kindness they had received from the members of the Parish." It was used to buy a plot of land for the cemetery, thus letting Catholic residents of Ypsi bury their loved ones nearby rather than fifteen to twenty miles away in Northville, where they had been sending them. According to Dennis Zimmer, in the fall 2006 edition of the *Ypsilanti Gleanings*, "The cemetery included a watch house, an eight foot square structure used by family members to guard at night against body snatchers who had an active trade with the University of Michigan medical school." That is correct, folks. The medical students of U of M often learned their trade on corpses stolen from the local cemeteries.

As the 1890s drew near, the Catholic population grew right alongside every other population in Ypsilanti. Combine that with the poor drainage of the area and a new cemetery was needed. Father William DeBever purchased the land on River Street, and as several cemeteries had done before, bodies were evacuated to the new location. But were all of them removed?

There are dormitories and a cafeteria/commons on top of the original St. John the Baptist Cemetery now, and a few of them come with their own tales of spooky experiences. There are theories that there was an Indigenous burial ground on campus as well, as one resident remembered the construction crew finding "old, old bones" while the old Pine Grove Terrace apartments were being constructed in the 1940s. These were demolished in the early aughts to make room for the Student Center.

To find out more about the original St. John's, head over to the section on Eastern Michigan University.

ALBAN CEMETERY

There is not much to the history of Alban Cemetery, which opened in 1885. Ypsilanti Township and the surrounding farmlands needed a cemetery, and one was created. The interesting part comes with the people who are buried there. John Burton, Ypsilanti's first Black mayor, was laid to rest there when he passed away in 1992 at eighty-one years old. He was elected mayor in 1967 and succeeded Ypsi's first female mayor, Sarah Sayre. Another big name in Ypsilanti's past resides there as well: Mrs. Whittaker.

The legend goes that Mrs. Whittaker (first name not included in any retellings) is buried at Alban Cemetery, but her spirit doesn't stay there. There is a large, white house down the road where the Whittakers used to live. Mrs. Whittaker hasn't been thrilled with how the house has been redecorated over the years, and she makes her presence known there. According to radio station WFMK, there are "doors that open and close by themselves, disembodied footsteps, pictures and paintings fall off walls and the appearance of a female apparition, believed by some to be the ghost of Mrs. Whittaker. She mostly appears in one of the upstairs rooms."

A commenter from the website Ghosts of America relates that they used to live in the Whittaker home in the 1990s. They posted, "Unexplained things happened in the house. Pictures flying across the room and breaking. 1800 style shoe prints in the newly finished hardwood floors. Doors opening and slamming shut on their own. I myself saw a ghostly figure standing in the window when I was upstairs doing homework."

There is no telling what happens within the walls of the old Whittaker home today, but one thing is for certain: no Whittakers are buried at Alban Cemetery. There are plenty in Highland Cemetery, but none was buried in the township. Could it still be the elusive Mrs. Whittaker? Absolutely. But she isn't strolling down the street from Alban!

WOODLAWN CEMETERY

Last, but certainly not least, this journey takes us to what is a small but still important cemetery in Ypsilanti, especially when talking about the area's Black history. Woodlawn Cemetery had a short life, operating from just 1946 to perhaps 1965, but its legacy is incredibly important to Ypsilanti's history. Incorporated in 1946 by Reverend Garther Roberson Sr., of the Second Baptist Church of Ypsilanti, it was meant for his congregation and the residents of that part of Ypsi that was, at the time, a predominantly Black neighborhood. According to Laura Bien in her article in the *Ann Arbor Chronicle* from 2013, this portion of Ypsilanti was redlined, a term coined from location maps that had neighborhoods of mostly people of color outlined in red ink, signifying "loan-worthiness" of neighborhoods for potential homebuyers. This often persuaded businesses and social services to not move into those neighborhoods, leaving people of color without basic amenities. Said Bien, "Often families, especially if new in town, lived several to a South Side home, another reality visible on old census forms. Ypsi banks would not give mortgages or even home improvement loans to black residents, a fact mentioned by…black residents."

The reverend died in 1955, and the cemetery was passed on to his wife, Estella Roberson, and a Mrs. Booker Rhonenee, but they

The field where Woodlawn Cemetery sits. *Kay Gray.*

declared bankruptcy not long after. There was no money set aside for the upkeep of the cemetery, and according to local historian James Mann, "The last burial in Woodlawn may have been in 1965. That same year the cemetery was abandoned."

Since then, it has fallen further and further into the forgotten places of Ypsi's memory. Some years ago, a fire destroyed the records of who is buried there, so now all anyone has to go on are a few more modern records of folks who have gone out in search of gravestones. These days, perhaps two to five stones are still visible. The rest of the cemetery has become overgrown, and without the plaque at the side of the road denoting that one is in Woodlawn, it looks like any other empty plot of land. It could use a good group of volunteers, ready with a lawnmower and some weed pullers, to pull it back into the light. It would be a shame to lose such an important piece of Ypsilanti's Black history.

This concludes the tour of Ypsilanti through its cemeteries. Cemeteries are a huge part of the human story, whether we like to think about them or not. May their stories live on to be told to the next generation, ghost stories and all.

Part II
Depot Town

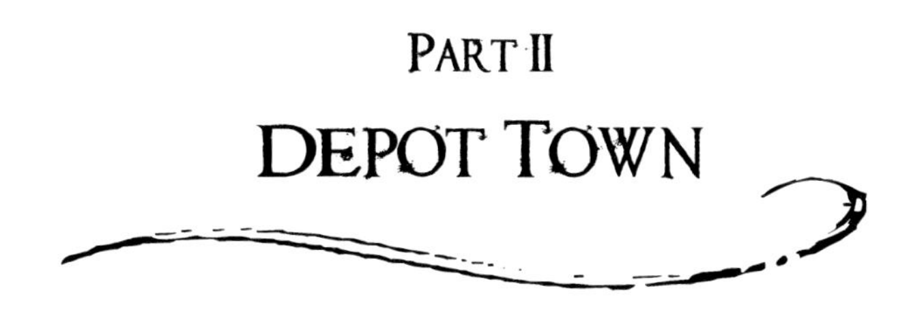

BRICK AND MORTAR MODERN GENERAL STORE

Depot Town's Brick and Mortar Modern General Store is one of a number of units that make up the old Follett House Hotel. Opened to the public on July 4, 1859, the Follett House was said to be the most luxurious hotel on the Michigan Central railway line. It was built by successful Ypsilanti banker and business owner Benjamin Follett. After serving as Ypsilanti's third mayor, Follett remained active in local politics as well as the growing community and purchased the equipment for the fire department, which he also helped to organize. It was also Benjamin Follett who persuaded the Michigan Central Railroad to build the depot in Ypsilanti in the 1850s.

Follett and his wife, Elvira Norris Follett, who was, among many other things, the first president of the Ypsilanti Ladies Library Association, together had seven children—five boys and two girls. Tragically, their second-youngest child, Mark Norris Follett, died at the age of six from diphtheria, just one year after the grandfather for whom he was named also passed. In the following year, 1864, Benjamin Follett himself passed away from an unknown disease of the lungs at the age of forty-five. His body, along with those of several of his relatives, was laid to rest at Highland Cemetery, which he had helped to found and was dedicated earlier that same year. Daughter Lucy also died young, only eighteen. Elvira Norris Follett continued to live an adventurous life with her children and grandchildren until 1884, when she died at the age of sixty-three. Her body was laid to rest beside her husband Benjamin's at Highland Cemetery.

The building that housed the Follett House also contained one of Benjamin Follett's banks along with law offices, various stores, a second-floor dining room and a ballroom on the top floor for theatrical performances and other social events. The pressed metal ceilings that were installed in the first floor retail spaces in the late 1800s or early 1900s are still visible today. It is not a surprise that the building was declared a historic structure by the Ypsilanti Heritage Foundation.

Follett sold his namesake building in 1864, although the hotel remained in operation under new ownership through the 1890s, after which it became a moccasin shoe factory. The Mayflower Cartage Company purchased the building in 1910 and used it as a storage facility until 1970. It was in these days that the walls that divided the first floor into individual shops were removed, although many have since been replaced as new stores have moved back into the mostly renovated building. The upper floors have largely been converted into apartments and studios.

Some of the businesses that moved in and out throughout the latter twentieth century include a delicatessen, a costume shop and a yoga studio. As of 2024, the businesses in operation are a thrift store, an art studio, an

The Follett House, date unknown. *Ypsilanti Historical Society.*

antiques shop and Brick and Mortar Modern General Store, which is owned and operated by Zachary and Sherri Schultz.

While they were moving into their new retail space back in 2016, the couple had a small party to celebrate the future opening of their store. Just a few friends, some drinks and good music in the otherwise empty space. Naturally, they took pictures to commemorate the occasion. In a few of those photos, a strange black, circular shadow showed up, almost as if it, too, was dancing with the happy new owners. It doesn't appear in all of the photos, nor is it in the same spot in every photo. There is another photo of the owners reflected in their back window. Off to the side, in the darkened space adjacent to the window, is a strange shape. One of the paranormal investigators who has been to Brick and Mortar thought that it may have been a woman with her hand up. The photo is tough to make out, but there is definitely some kind of distortion in the dark space.

An interesting note that a few of our locations have pointed out is that a lot of the spirits in Ypsilanti seem to wander. Sherri said that she was "told by someone else who had come in…that they felt like there was a woman in an apron who does her rounds in Depot Town, cleaning." Similarly, there are a few ghosts that walk through several stores downtown, in what was once the Occidental Hotel. Ypsi is a busy place!

Zachary and Sherri's dog, Dave, also has a favorite spot to lie down that's not at his owners' side. Dave enjoys the occasional nap toward the front of the store, by one of the large front windows. A psychic visiting the shop for a paranormal investigation back in November 2022 claimed that there may be a child spirit hanging around the shop that is drawn to Dave. "Dave will always be at my feet," Sherri said. "Occasionally, he'll walk up to the front corner and just lay down over there. Apparently there might be an eight-year-old boy that really likes him." The child lingers around that front area where Dave sleeps. Dowsing rods used during the investigation conducted by the Plymouth Ghost Hunters seemed to corroborate that there is a little boy in the shop.

During their investigation, Plymouth Ghost Hunters heard several names coming through their spirit box while doing a question-and-answer session in the basement. "Dave" came through clearly, and when asked their names, the spirits seemed to say "Ian" and "Marie." Upstairs on the main floor, during another session with the spirit box, the investigators asked for confirmation that there was someone with them who was in the Civil War. They received an affirmative. They asked the person's name, and through the box came the name "Murray." "Zach" even came up all on its own.

A black mass can be seen in only a few photos from the evening. *Sherri Schultz.*

What is very interesting is that the voices are all different. There isn't one tone, and they range between masculine- and feminine-sounding. And the investigators didn't just get answers through the spirit box. They also conducted EVP sessions, and the responses were even clearer. At one point, someone or something said "band saw" in the basement, where Zachary's woodshop is located. (The highlights of the investigation can be viewed for free on YouTube.)

It looked to be a very fruitful investigation, and Brick and Mortar appears to have several spirits that call the location home, in addition to the wandering ghosts that visit a number of other places in Depot Town.

THIS, THAT AND THE ODDER THINGS

This, That and the Odder Things is one of the businesses that makes up the Masonic Block along with Sidetrack Bar and Grill, the Hair Station and Depot Town Cats and Dogs. The building has always been home to myriad businesses on the street level and apartments overtop. It was also the original home for Ypsilanti's Masons. The third floor of the western portion of the building was once the location of the first Masonic Temple. After the Masons moved to their newly built home in 1909 on Huron Street (now the Riverside Arts Center), another fraternal organization, the Knights of the Maccabees, later simply called the Maccabees, took over the space.

It seems that it is not so much the building that is haunted, although it does have a unique ambience, but rather the objects that Claire Broderick, the shop's owner, brings into it. A number of antique items have come and gone from the store, and all of them have stories to tell. For instance, there is a clown cabinet that sits at the front of the store that can best be described as "creepy." At about three feet tall, with the head of a jester poking out of the top, feet supporting it all on the bottom and doors that don't quite stay shut, the small cabinet is startling at first glance. Its eyes look like they might follow you around the room, and according to Claire, the entire head may turn to stare.

"I have felt him watching and have questioned, 'Did his head move?'" she said. It hasn't repeated the performance with anyone paying attention, but it does give off an eerie feeling when looked at. Those penetrating eyes don't help. Its origin only adds to its odd tale. "He was found somewhere on the street in Ypsi. Some house around here had him," explained Claire. "And my neighbor just saw it and was like, 'Oh, I'm gonna pick that up for Claire.' And you know, he was obviously hand-carved." And as of the writing of this book, the jester cabinet sits by the front door of This, That and the Odder Things, waiting to be taken home by some unsuspecting curio collector.

But that isn't the only thing bringing the odd vibes into the shop. The nature of This, That and the Odder Things being on the eclectic side, items of that nature find their way into Claire's hands. This includes three human skulls passing through the shop at different times. One was in a sealed box lined with LED lights. One day, in front of one of the shop's employees, the lights began to pulse. Slowly the LEDs pulsed on and off, on and off. The boxed skull only did this once, but it was enough to produce a sense of unease in both Claire and the employee.

"It was just a different kind of energy, not a flicker, right? But it would slowly [pulse]. And…one particular employee actually was like, 'Claire, I think this is haunted. Do you know anything about the skull?' And I was like, 'Well, I got it in an estate sale from a doctor, but I don't really know the history.'" That skull is no longer in the store.

The clown cabinet that possibly moves. *Kay Gray*.

The other two skulls never provided as much activity as the first, but it is still incredibly rare to find human bones for sale due to the strict regulations put on the handling of human remains. However, it is completely legal, and curio shops do have them occasionally. One of the skulls that passed through

This, That and the Odder Things had been used for medical teaching and was quite old. It was cut into pieces that could be removed and examined. The origins of the other were slightly more dubious. Claire declined to have much to do with it, but she did say that it was "the creepiest," in part due to how she suspected it was cleaned: the natural way, with dirt, insects and bacteria in the ground.

Surely, those won't be the only strange objects to pass through the store. If you're looking for possibly haunted objects to start or add to your collection, This, That and the Odder Things is the place to go.

THE THOMPSON BLOCK

Originally known as the Norris Block, after Mark Norris, one of the men who basically created Depot Town, the Thompson Block has stood on the corner of Cross and River Streets since 1860. According to James Mann, "The new building, a three story Italianate structure, was planned for both retail and residential use. The ground floor was designed for six retail shops." Incredible to think that Ypsilanti has always had mixed-use buildings!

Because the building was constructed on the opposite side of the railroad tracks from the railroad depot, tunnels were built that ran under the tracks and connected some of the basements of buildings on Cross Street; the Norris Block, as it was then called; and the depot. This made it easier to move things around without interfering with the busy rails. Local legend claims that freedom seekers who had fled slavery in the South hid in these tunnels during the day. Abolitionists Leonard and Elizabeth Chase lived nearby and were known to hide freedom seekers in their home. They and others may have used these tunnels to get people to the Huron River, where boats would have transported them farther east.

Only a year after its construction, the very large building was turned over to be used as barracks for the 14th and 27th Michigan Infantries, housing men while they trained before being sent to the front lines. The block became known as "The Barracks" for many years after.

The Norris Block wouldn't take the name of Oliver E. Thompson until several years after he bought the property in 1869. He opened a paint factory and store and, over the years, expanded into making and selling wagons, carriages and eventually invented and sold his own farm equipment. According to James Mann, Thompson and his sons sold more

The Thompson Block under the ownership of O.E. Thompson. *Ypsilanti Historical Society.*

than two hundred bicycles in one year. That's great business! Thompson and Sons also rented out several of the shops for other businesses, and even the volunteer fire department was housed there in the 1890s.

In 1916, Thompson's grandson Joseph opened what may have been the first Dodge dealership outside Detroit. They, of course, sold the first Dodge car made, the 30-35 Touring Car. The Thompson Block continued to serve the community in one way or another until about 1950, when the last of the businesses left and the building was vacated. It was bought by David Kircher in 1960, but it was no more than storage. Nothing was done to keep up the building until 1996, when a court order was issued demanding Kircher repair the building, as he was "guilty of demolishing the Thompson Block building by neglect." By the early 2000s, the Thompson Block was put under receivership and awarded to local real estate company Barnes and Barnes, which did the majority of repairs. Because Kircher had failed to pay, the block was put into the hands of Barnes and Barnes and then sold to Stewart Beal (another real estate mogul in Ypsilanti) around 2006.

And then, on September 23, 2009, tragedy struck the historic building. At 1:40 a.m., a fire broke out somewhere on the second floor of the constantly-under-construction building. Firefighters arrived on the scene very shortly thereafter, but a building as big as the Thompson, with so much unfinished and open, was merely kindling. The *Ann Arbor News* reported at the time, "Ypsilanti fire officials said the building, which was being remodeled for lofts and retail space, was significantly damaged. A part of the building's roof collapsed." It took several fire departments from the area to finally put the fire out.

Officials declared the fire as intentional. "Ypsilanti Fire Inspector John Roe said it doesn't appear to be accidental. 'I don't suspect this fire started by accident,' he said. 'Accidental fires of this nature would not burn that quickly.'" When all was said and done, only the outer façade of the old building was left standing.

Still owned by Stewart Beal at the time, there was speculation that the fire started because there was construction happening even after the proper permit had expired months before. But in 2010, investigations determined the fire to be arson and the possible perpetrator to be Jacob Popiolek. A warrant was put out for his arrest, and he was subsequently caught and given a trial. He pleaded no contest to setting the fire, having been in the empty building with friends that night, drinking and smoking. He was sentenced to five years' probation but skipped out on paying restitution to Beal. A new warrant for his arrest was issued in 2015. However, the information trail stops there.

Sadly, this isn't the last tragedy to befall the Thompson Block. Jeremy Burd was working with others in the basement of the building in May 2015 when

"The Barracks," which housed Michigan infantries during the Civil War. *Ypsilanti Historical Society.*

The morning after the 2009 fire. *Ypsilanti Historical Society*.

he struck the joists supporting the first floor, causing the floor to crash down on him. He was declared dead upon arriving at St. Joseph Mercy Hospital in Ypsilanti. An investigation was immediately conducted, and ultimately five citations were issued to Beal Construction by the Michigan Occupational Safety and Health Administration (MIOSHA) for serious violations. "The five citations describe a construction site that was not properly prepared, inspected or cleared including during the time when Burd was killed," MLive wrote. There had been a pile of wood just above the workers, on the first floor, that should have been moved prior to work being done in the basement. It fell onto Burd along with the first floor itself. A witness and coworker there that morning told MLive that Beal Construction had been informed of the concerns of having the pile of wood on the first floor, but no plans were made to move it.

It took until 2021 for the Thompson Block to be completed and start a new life. Thompson & Co., a restaurant inspired by southern home cooking and named for the building, opened on the first floor in August 2021. Mash Bar, serving unique whiskey-based cocktails and classics, joined it not long after, and together they offer a cozy-yet-classic atmosphere to enjoy a drink and a meal. As posted on Thompson & Co.'s website, "With a rich history that was once of such importance, it feels just to bring the Thompson Block back to life. Stationed at the end of depot town, Thompson & Co. strives to create a place for community to meet."

It may come as no surprise that Thompson & Co. and Mash Bar have their fair share of paranormal stories. After all, as they said, the Thompson Block was a place for community in one way or another, and it seems that both the living and not stop in for fellowship and perhaps a little mischief. In general, employees have described the feeling of being watched whenever they are in the building. This feeling is much stronger on the Thompson & Co. side than the Mash side, and one employee described walking through the swinging doors between businesses as "eerie as hell." One theory as to why the building is haunted is that whoever or whatever is still in the block may be angry that the building has been almost completely reconstructed and most certainly has been changed from how it appeared before the fire in 2009. The other may be caused by the tragedy of the construction worker who died on site.

One bartender said that when strange things happen around the bar, they blame "Mr. Norris." Perhaps the funniest part is that they had no idea who Mr. Norris was, just that there used to be a drink named after him, and he somehow became the ghost! They even named a skeleton used for décor at Halloween Mr. Norris.

The basement is especially spooky, as it seems most of the basements in Ypsilanti are. The bartender described the area where the worker died during the rebuild of the block as being the creepiest section. They will go out of their way to avoid that area of the basement. Another server said she had heard "footsteps running up and down the stairs" of the basement while she was down there. This has happened more than once. Employees also find the bathrooms to be unsettling and have experienced the lights flickering in them on more than once occasion.

With love and maybe a little luck, the Thompson Block will continue being a part of the Ypsilanti community for decades to come. That includes residents, employees *and* ghosts.

THE UNSOLVED MURDER OF RICHARD STREICHER

Whoever the killer was, they were thorough in both their actions and their escape. The body of Richard J. Streicher, seven years old, was found on a cold March day in Ypsilanti in 1935. He had been stabbed fourteen times with a sharp instrument, although it was determined that the first three, to the heart, were the ones that killed him. The others were to the head and neck. He had been beaten with a blunt instrument as well, and officials suspected that he had been submerged in the Huron River after his death.

Richard's body was found by thirteen-year-old Buck Holt, who noticed small tracks going under the footbridge that spanned over the river from Cross Street to Frog Island Park, then known as Island Park. Holt thought the tracks belonged to a muskrat, and he followed them to investigate. Unfortunately, instead of a muskrat, Holt found Richard's body lying on a small dirt outcropping. He immediately went for help.

There were no easily discovered clues left behind. Combined with the news spreading like wildfire across the small city, which led to curious onlookers crowding the area, authorities had nothing to go off besides the boy's body itself. This led to a few interesting early theories. "Prosecutor Albert J. Rapp," wrote the *Ann Arbor News* at the time, "said the number of stab wounds in the chest and head of the young victim indicated the killing was 'the work of a frenzied sex maniac,' but admitted that no suspects had been found." Dr. Stacy C. Howard, a pathologist at St. Joseph Mercy Hospital, agreed with Rapp, telling the *Ann Arbor News* in a different article that "the nature of the crime tended to show the slayer was a sex pervert." However, the *News* made sure to add that Dr. Howard "refused to explain his belief."

Captain Donald S. Leonard of the Detroit police said that it was likely to be a revenge killing, which Richard's mother, Lucia Streicher, agreed with. Mrs. Streicher was the daughter of a wealthy engineer, and she claimed he had made many enemies over the years. Mr. Richard Streicher's father owned the family business, Streicher Tool & Die Company, and suggested that someone may want revenge against the family for ill will from that side. There was also a divorced uncle in the family who may have wanted revenge on the Streichers for earlier business. The uncle was brought in but ultimately let go and dismissed as a suspect.

Five days into the investigation, everyone who could have possibly seen Richard the day he was murdered had been questioned twice. His parents had told officers that they last saw Richard around 4:30 p.m. the day before, when he told them he was going out to play. At around 7:40 p.m., they contacted the authorities after unsuccessfully looking for Richard near their home. They also described Richard's sled being returned to the home by someone who was not Richard. Lucia knew this because it was leaning at an angle unlike the usual one Richard left it at. Some of Richard's friends, including a George Young, told officers about how they played with Richard around 4:00 p.m.

The footbridge under which Richard Streicher's body was found. *Ypsilanti Historical Society.*

that afternoon, sledding down a nearby hill. According to the *Ann Arbor News*, "Young told police that at about 4:30 Richard walked off with a tall man dressed in a black overcoat." But still authorities had no leads.

They questioned and ultimately let go twelve "degenerates," men from Ypsilanti to Detroit, who had reputations that led officers to believe them capable of such a heinous crime. Officers questioned Richard's parents again. They lamented losing the possible evidence that might have been found on Richard's clothing, as they were burned by the funeral home almost immediately after Richard's body was brought in on Mrs. Streicher's orders.

In a fashion similar to the Michigan Murders, a psychic soon got involved. In August 1935, Mrs. Fred Gordon got in touch with Police Chief Southard saying that she had read the news about the murder and thought she could determine if Lucia was guilty. Mrs. Streicher reluctantly agreed to be seen by the psychic, going into the meeting with a skeptical mind. But she came out sobbing. According to Gregory Fournier in his book, *The Richard J. Streicher Murder: Ypsilanti's Depot Town Mystery*, "Lucia told them the psychic revealed her son was in the basement of the hatchery and was killed by a man who worked there." She provided the gruesome details, including that a knife was buried along the bank of the Huron River. She blamed Frederick Leighton, owner of the Neuhauser Chicken Hatchery, over and over and over again, completely certain that it was him. These details would lead authorities exactly nowhere.

Then in stepped a man named Clinton I. LeForge. LeForge, lawyer from Ypsilanti and whose family has a street and nature preserve named for them in the area, had been "investigating" the crime from moment one, claiming that he "was a special deputy sheriff, and interested in criminal work." He offered several "tips" to the authorities. LeForge also confessed that he knew the Streichers. He had worked for Lucia in 1933 and drew up divorce papers that were never filed. They were pending at the time of the murder but canceled by Lucia after learning of her son's death.

Two years later, with dozens of suspects let go and still no leads in the case, Circuit Judge George Sample called for a one-man grand jury, telling the *Ann Arbor News* that "he expressed a desire to put an end to 'intense feeling and suspicion within the community.'" The Streichers were the first in a long line of people to testify. LeForge was called up to testify, and it was noted in the paper that in 1936 he was disbarred for misusing funds of an estate for which he was administrator. The papers were sure to point out that little detail just about every time they mentioned him. But even the grand jury didn't bring anything to light. No, that would be a series of letters sent to authorities from neighbors, friends and a census taker that gossiped about Lucia's real personality.

Gregory Fournier published a few of these letters. They describe a very different Streicher family from what the *Ann Arbor News* portrayed. The census taker was with Lucia the afternoon of Richard's murder. "Mrs. Streicher was irritable with a headache and possibly struck her son," the letter says. "Maybe she hit him harder than she thought and had to finish the job to cover up her bad temper." Both the census taker and new neighbors, the Murrays, described Lucia hitting her son both on the day of the murder and a week before. Several neighbors, including those living in the same house as the family, described to Police Chief Southard overhearing a heated argument between Richard's parents the day of the murder. The Streichers denied such a thing when confronted about it.

The letters also frequently brought up LeForge. "The Murrays claimed Lucia told them she was pregnant with Clinton LeForge's baby. She added that LeForge was her lawyer," Fournier wrote. A few other neighbors wrote to Southard that they had seen LeForge go into Mrs. Streicher's home often and that Lucia asked him to remove all Richard's toys from his room the day after he was murdered. However, when he was brought in for questioning and asked about his romantic involvement with Mrs. Streicher, he vehemently denied it, saying, "Never! That woman is hell!...I couldn't live with that woman for five minutes! I don't know how Dick stands it." He left the police station with a solid alibi for the night of the murder.

It seems that at the time, half the neighborhood believed Lucia to be capable of murder even if she hadn't outright done it. But what was uncovered over the course of the grand jury and the questioning of more than forty witnesses was little more than nailing down the last time anyone saw Richard (around 5:15 p.m.) and all of the people who *couldn't* have killed him. Three years after the murder, there were no suspects, no motive and no murder weapon.

Lucia Streicher became more and more suspicious. She and her husband were questioned several more times, together and separately, but never did their story change or even waver from each other's. It seemed that prosecutor Rapp believed Lucia to be the murderer as well, with LeForge possibly involved, but he just couldn't find enough solid evidence to convict her.

There is more to the story than this. But ultimately no one was ever indicted or even arrested. No instrument of murder was found. No one could be fully pinned for the murder of a seven-year-old boy who went out to sled one March afternoon and never returned home.

Clint LeForge and Richard are interred at Highland Cemetery. Richard wasn't given a memorial stone until 2016. In 2015, MLive released an article on the cold case, which drove the Ypsilanti Historical Society to begin looking for more clues and gave John Sisk, a resident of Jackson and the manager of a St. Vincent de Paul thrift store, an idea. He started a GoFundMe to raise money for a gravestone, and the community pitched in. "I am so grateful for the people in this area for taking their time and donating their money to help reach this goal," Sisk said in MLive. "Hopefully, wherever [Streicher's] at, he's smiling."

On October 15, 2016, a funeral service was held for Richard. About thirty people showed up to pay their respects to a boy who has never been forgotten in the community. The headstone reads, "Always remembered, never forgotten." There is a sled etched into it to remember the joy he had before his life was cut tragically short.

THE FROG, THE MYTH, THE LEGEND

Did you know that Ypsilanti has its very own cryptid? There is a legend that started in Riverside Park that has captivated residents for ages. Well, all right. Maybe not captivated. But it sure has confused a lot of people who visit the park and wonder what on earth that plaque is talking about. Just what exactly is a "Smeet Frog"?

Artist's depiction of the Smeet Frog. *Ypsilanti Historical Society*.

The first sign dedicated to this mysterious maybe-amphibian showed up at the Tridge (the place where the three pedestrian bridges under Cross Street meet over the Huron River) in 1999. Apparently posted by the Ypsilanti Hysterical Society, this plaque told of the Smeet Frog, a furred frog with the ability to fly. Native to the Huron River, and only found there, Smeet was said to be a winter staple of the Indigenous peoples who stopped in the area. Its fur gets coated in moss easily, making it incredibly difficult to see, especially as it is only active at night. It used to number in the thousands, but its population has declined. Smeet is a protected species these days, and hunting it is illegal. Or so said the initial plaque.

That was unfortunately removed by city workers, but another was put in its place shortly thereafter—and with new information! The Smeet Frog is migratory, using its ability to fly to leave the presumably-too-hot summer of Riverside Park for the milder land of Labrador. You know, as amphibians are wont to do.

Apparently this legend made a few teachers quite angry with Ypsilanti. Younger students asked a few of the nearby universities about Smeet, wondering if it was actually real. One teacher from the Detroit area was so upset that she "wrote an acerbic letter to local editors decrying the practice of telling lies to children. Fables of Santa Claus, the Easter Bunny, and the

Tooth Fairy notwithstanding, she was irate and pledged to never again bring her students to Ypsilanti."

The second plaque faded and molded with time, and it, too, was removed. A third popped up sometime around 2010 but was also removed for reasons unknown. In 2013, a brand-new plaque was placed on the Tridge in honor of Tom Dodd, local historian and avid activist for the underserved in the community. Unfortunately, there is no plaque anymore (as of 2023), but hopefully in the future another will be placed, so that all may learn of this very, very elusive species.

Plaque or not, the Legend of the Smeet Frog lives on. Dreamland Theater did an entire puppet show about it. It can be found in a few of the Neighborhood Theatre Group's performances, including *Annie Ypsi and the Case of the Missing Smeet*, a short film written by A.M. Dean and Kristin Anne Danko that is available on YouTube, and *Dispatches from the Dumb Decade*, a musical also written by A.M. Dean, among others. Ypsi Alehouse created an IPA to honor the Smeet called Backyard Frog. There are stickers, buttons, shirts and almost any kind of merchandise one could

"The Tridge," where the plaque dedicated to the Smeet Frog once stood. *Kay Gray.*

want with Ypsilanti's famous beast on them. Back in 2022, he also ran for mayor of Ypsi! There was even an entire festival in 2023 dedicated to the legend.

So, the next time you find yourself in Riverside Park, be sure to keep an eye out for Ypsi's favorite cryptid, the Smeet Frog!

INTERLUDE

MINI MYSTERIES

RAWSONVILLE GHOST TOWN

At the bottom of Grove Street, at just about the border of Ypsilanti Charter Township and Van Buren Township, sits a plaque. Out in front of a McDonald's, on a busy street, it's very easy to miss, but if you were to find parking and take a look, you'd discover that you were on the ground of what used to be Rawsonville, a little town from our past that is now long gone. You can still see it! Well, you can see where it once was. For below Belleville Lake some of it sits, forever entombed in water thanks to the efforts of the Michigan Central Railroad and the Detroit Edison Company.

Dubbed Snow's Landing in 1823 by Henry Snow, the first man to settle the area (for the Americans, that is), the town of Rawsonville itself was officially founded as Michigan City by Amariah Rawson in 1836. The name was changed to Rawsonville in 1838 after a petition by Rawson to the state legislature was approved.

It was a booming little town, complete with its own post office, sawmill, gristmill and stove factory. Rawsonville also boasted three whole saloons to slake the thirst of all those hardworking employees. This was big business for the 1860s, when the town hit its peak. Mike Safoutin, author of the article "Old Rawsonville: Setting the Record Straight," did a deep search into the actual boundary lines of the little village and found some exciting information: "The businesses were concentrated primarily in about three blocks running along

The historical marker for Rawsonville, sitting between two fast-food restaurants. *Kay Gray.*

both sides of today's Rawsonville Road....They would have been detached wooden structures, not continuous brick storefronts." So it looked a lot more like a Wild West town than the brick-and-mortar buildings we still see in downtown Ypsilanti and Depot Town.

Unfortunately, the town was destined for failure. When the railroad came to the area, it bypassed Rawsonville completely, instead setting its eyes on the little village of Ypsilanti. That was the beginning of the end. With traffic now going around the town rather than through it, and Belleville to one side and Ypsilanti on the other, Rawsonville saw its businesses and residents move away over the course of the next fifty years. In 1895, the post office was moved to Van Buren Township, although it did come back for a short time. But by 1902, it was gone again and never returned.

And then the Detroit Edison Company, better known as DTE, came onto the scene and decided that the Huron River would be a great place for a dam. It bought the land on which Rawsonville sat in 1910, which by then was home to nearly no one, and built the French Landing hydroelectric dam in 1925. The diversion of the Huron River created Belleville Lake—and sank a small portion of the village. It doesn't seem to have ever reached the businesses that lined the old Michigan Avenue, but it very well may have covered up individual homes that were not on any platted maps of the region. There were, however, a few vestiges of the old town left to visit in recent history. Again from the article "Old Rawsonville": "Old timers may remember the original Rawsonville Inn building, a remnant of the original town, that stood at this location until sometime in the 1960s, when it was demolished to make more room for the widening of Rawsonville Road." Another piece of history taken away to make room for bigger and better.

Now you can sail on top of a ghost town, or at least part of one, somewhere beneath the waters of Belleville Lake, lost to progression and innovation. No word on if the lake is haunted, however. But it may be worth checking out on a sunny afternoon in July.

THE BONES UNDER BELL STREET

It was a normal day in 1933 when Thomas Smith of the Ypsilanti Water Company went to work digging a new trench in the center of Bell Street. The intention was to replace the old water main with a new one, and so that's what the Water Company was doing that morning—until Smith came across something very strange.

Sitting above the old water main was a very old box containing some very old bones. Confused and mildly alarmed, Smith took the bones from the hole and delivered them to Dr. J.J. Woods of Ypsilanti. He determined them to have been buried "for no more than 50 years." Dr. W.B. Hinsdale, professor of anthropology at the University of Michigan, later got his hands on them. The people the bones belonged to could have been victims of a murder, all stuffed in the same box to try to conceal the deed. It was briefly speculated that there could have been an Indigenous burial ground there, but no other bodies had been found in the digging of the trench.

Hinsdale concluded that "the remains were of four persons, two men, a woman and a child. He was able to determine there were four bodies in the grave, by the thickness of the fragments of the skulls." It was related that the doctor was annoyed, however, that the remains had been taken from the trench, making further analysis much more difficult. "No implements, jewelry or other trinkets were found with the bones, and their position in the earth led to the belief that the bodies may have been crowded into a small box in a cramped position and buried in that way," wrote the *Ypsilanti Daily Press* from January 19, 1933. But being unable to investigate the location as it was when the bodies were found, there wasn't much more that could have been done.

More theories abounded. They could have been Indigenous, as the Native people from the area often buried their dead in mounds and other multi-person graves. In fact, Hinsdale had originally come to Ypsilanti to study said mounds. Another theory was that they were victims of the smallpox epidemic that struck Ypsilanti in the 1830s.

Unfortunately, only one lead was given. "Robert Simons… explained, the bones were first uncovered some thirty-five years earlier, perhaps in 1896, when workmen installed the water main. He had been the foreman of the crew who had found the bones in the center of the street." Instead of calling authorities to examine the bones, they were tossed in a box and reburied, this time on top of the newly installed water main.

At least half the mystery was solved, but the other went unexplained. To this day, no one knows who the people were, where they came from or how they died. However, there have been some spooky happenings on Bell Street that could be the spirits of the past coming to call. The website Ghosts of America has a collection of personal ghost stories from people all over the country. A few of them have something to say about their homes on Bell Street. One commenter saw an apparition of a girl in the living room and shadows by the upstairs windows and even had someone or something lie in bed with them and touch their side. They turned to see no one else in the room, let alone the bed. This was corroborated by another commenter on the website, who claims to have lived in the same house. Apparitions were seen, toys were thrown around and "once I was in the master bedroom and got a burning sensation on my arm. A burning sensation enough to make me look at my arm where I found a freshly scratched mark about 3 inches long."

Who knows what or who else might be buried under Bell Street.

CAFÉ LUWAK

Back when 42 Cross Street was Café Luwak (named after kopi luwak, also known as civet coffee)—which served espresso,

Number 42 East Cross Street stands empty, save for its ghosts. *Kay Gray*.

sandwiches and ice cream—local psychic and teacher Beverly Fish met every Thursday with a small group of like-minded folk. "We either did readings or whatever people wanted," she said. "Runes, or I did astrology. We did all kinds of things." This included occasionally channeling.

One night, they met a female spirit. Said Fish, "I called her something weird because I didn't like her, and she didn't like me, and so I made some name up for her. And she didn't like my friend because she is from Holland, and she sounded like a German person."

Fish explained that the spirit was from the World War I era, when anti-German sentiment was high. The spirit ended up pushing Fish's friend's coffee cup into her lap. Another time, the spirit shoved a set of salt and pepper shakers onto the floor.

One night, the spirit was agitated and wanted to go to the basement. Fish said, "She was really mad, and so I went. I said, okay, I'll go down there. Show me what you want to show me." It turned out that "her stairway to go upstairs was no longer there, and she was mad because she used to live upstairs in the apartments." The spirit was so angry about this injustice that "she would throw things around."

Fish also revealed that the woman had been a sex worker. This may have been corroborated by Joseph H. Thompson and his memories of early twentieth-century Depot Town, which were published in the July 1974 issue of the Ypsilanti Historical Society's publication, *Ypsilanti Gleanings*. Thompson recalled an establishment people referred to as the "horse exchange" where gamblers placed bets on horse races. Above this was "a house of ill-repute" run by a woman named "Ma" Bush. It isn't entirely clear if Thompson was referring to the building where Fish met the former sex worker or the building next door, but it would seem that these two stories do line up.

There has been no word on whether or not this spirit bothered patrons at the Café Ollie or Ollie Food and Spirits, the businesses that followed Café Luwak at 42 Cross. According to Fish, being a human spirit, the former sex worker can come and go whenever she pleases, even if the space is cleansed or "exorcized."

THE YPSILANTI WATER TOWER

Although Ypsilanti's stone water tower itself is not a mystery, there have been a number of legends associated with it over the years that make it worthy of making an appearance in this book. After all, how can one not think of its infamous silhouette when discussing the city? Its likeness is found on T-shirts, bags, bumper stickers and postcards, and it has been turned into candles, stuffed pillows and bar taps all across the region. Completed in 1890, the water tower was made with Joliet limestone (so named because of the area in Illinois where it comes from) and wooden shingles, done in the popular Queen Anne style of architecture, and stands 147 feet tall. The steel tank holds up to 250,000 gallons. It was built at the highest point in the city, which these days unfortunately means modern buildings have covered up the view of it from several angles. However, locals still use it as a convenient landmark in order to direct people around the city.

The water tower has been in continuous use since 1890, and it was the city's only water tower until the 1950s. Since 1974, it has been maintained by the Ypsilanti Community Utilities Authority. The tower has received several honors over its century-plus of life, including being declared an American Water Landmark in 1975 and a National Historic Landmark in the 1980s, as well as earning the "most phallic building in the world" award from *Cabinet Magazine* in 2003. In fact, locals often lovingly refer to the water tower as "the Brick Dick."

One of the first legends associated with the tower has to do with the crosses built into the walls. While the real reason is relatively simple, folks who may not know the history of the tower's construction still enjoy speculation. Rumors of the tower being a part of some secret society ritual have made their way through the city. The truth is that the superstitious day laborers who built the water tower added at minimum three crosses inside and outside to help protect themselves from harm during construction. One of them is visible from the outside above the door on the west side of the tower. These additions were said to enrage the architect, William R. Coats. But by the time he discovered what had been changed, it was too late to do anything about it. Whether it was thanks to the holy protection the crosses were intended to provide or just good building practices, no accidents happened during the tower's construction.

The Ypsilanti Water Tower also sits directly across the street from Eastern Michigan University. So, of course, it has become part of the lore of the university as well. Legend has it that should someone ever graduate from EMU still a virgin, the water tower will crumble and fall. Seeing as it has stood strong and proud since 1890, either EMU students have taken that legend seriously, or it's not as true as it claims. Either way, the Ypsi Water Tower will always have a special place in the hearts of locals and visitors for years to come. Its beloved nature is why it made the cover of this book as well.

THE GIRL ON THE BIKE

An employee from the Ann Arbor District Library brought a question to the *Haunted Mitten* podcast: Did they know anything about the little girl on a bike that their partner and sister-in-law had seen a few times driving through the more rural parts of Ypsilanti? At the intersection of Ridge and Hack Roads, just outside Ypsilanti Charter Township, these folks have seen what they believe to be a girl in 1940s or 1950s clothing riding a bicycle. After dark. By herself. And they haven't seen her just once. At least twice on their journey back to Ann Arbor they have seen the girl riding her bike alone in the evening.

Digging through the cemeteries in the area (pun intended) and then searching through old newspaper archives turned up no one matching the description having passed away within the time frame the clothing suggests. But this part of the county is very rural, and so any number of things could have happened in the past that weren't necessarily documented. And if they were, the records weren't necessarily kept this long. This is also not to say that someone had to have died in an area to haunt it. Perhaps this little girl loved riding her bicycle there so much that her spirit has chosen to repeat the beloved activity.

Another theory concerns a time slip, in which our present time and another (past or future) time overlap. Perhaps these two keep experiencing a moment out of time, as if the veil there is thinner than other places. It's a mystery if anyone else has seen the little girl riding after dark on this lonely stretch of road.

Part III
Around Town

MICHIGAN FIREHOUSE MUSEUM AND EDUCATION CENTER

In 2023, Ypsilanti celebrated its bicentennial anniversary. At the same time, two icons of the community celebrated their 125th and 25th anniversaries as well. The Michigan Firehouse Museum and Education Center is located on the corners of Huron and Cross Streets and serves as one of Ypsi's most prominent windows to its past.

The firehouse itself isn't Ypsilanti's first, but it still has quite a history, having been built by the city in 1898 and stayed in use right up until 1975. It is built out of gorgeous red brick, and its bright-red garage doors signal what this building was used for well before you see the sign.

According to Dave Egeler, the Firehouse Museum's director of operations, before the firehouse reopened as the museum, it was home to a plumbing company. Howard and Norma Weaver, the museum's founders, purchased the property in 1998 with the intention of turning it into a museum. "Mrs. Weaver's dad [Henry Clement] was an Ann Arbor firefighter who died in the line of duty," Egeler explained. The Weavers were local business owners as well as great collectors of antique vehicles, including vintage fire trucks and pumpers. The majority of the items now on display were generously donated by the family. Both Howard and Norma Weaver have passed away, but their love of firefighting history lives on.

The original 1898 firehouse side of the museum has been set to look very much as it did before it closed, and it was opened to the public as a

The original firehouse in its heyday. *Ypsilanti Historical Society*.

museum in 1999. The large multilevel exhibit space was added in 2002 and now houses numerous vintage fire trucks and other firefighting tools, such as fire extinguishers, bells, ladders, gear and more, some of which date back to the nineteenth century. According to Tripadvisor, the museum is the third-most popular attraction in Ypsilanti, which means it is well worth a visit if you are in the area.

Every website on ghosts seems to tell the same story: Alonzo Miller, fire chief from the early 1900s, died in the line of duty in 1922. It is his spirit that haunts the Firehouse Museum, unable or unwilling to leave his life's work behind. However, Chief Miller did not die in that fire or any fire. In fact, he lived until 1940. His family debunked the myth themselves, but this hasn't stopped the legend from persisting. It also hasn't stopped people from experiencing strange things in the historic building or seeking them out. Dave Egeler provided some backstory to the legend:

> *In 1941 firefighters were using this Firehouse and living here.…Firefighters started saying that they thought that the place was haunted. It was Alonzo Miller who's coming back and, you know, it was a year after he had passed. But the firefighters were reporting that they thought he was visiting them. That* [may have] *started as a joke, and it just kind of carried forward. I mean, this building creaks and moans and it's noisy…the only information I have is a statement that says firefighters were reporting in 1941 they thought he was haunting the place.*

It may have been that they genuinely thought Miller hadn't left the firehouse where he had spent his career. It could have also started as a joke one night and spiraled into the urban legend we know it as today. Either way, the myth of Miller dying in a fire at the firehouse can be put to bed. What can't be, however, is that strange things are still being experienced.

Beverly Fish—psychic, medium and one of the readers at the nearby metaphysical store Evenstar's Chalice—has had her own experience with who she believes to be Fire Chief Miller. In fact, he followed her home after a meeting to discuss the paranormal convention the Firehouse Museum held back in 2018, as well as Fish doing psychic readings during the event. "And then Alonzo appeared," Fish said about being inside the museum. "And I thought, 'Oh, okay.' So then I went out to my car, and the alarm was going off. How did that happen? Because I don't have a chip. And so I thought, 'He's doing that!' I knew it was him. I said, 'Stop that,' and it stopped. So I went home, and then different things happened. I thought, 'Okay, you need

Chief Miller stands second on the left with the 1936 Ypsilanti Fire Department. *Ypsilanti Historical Society.*

to go back to the fire station. You gotta go.'" And he must have listened to her because Fish hasn't had him in her home since.

The museum occasionally opens its doors to investigation groups, and they have caught some compelling evidence over the years. As well as getting hits on a REM pod (a device that emits electromagnetic energy and makes an ungodly noise when it detects something—or someone—disturb the energy field), investigators have captured stick figures through a camera akin to an Xbox Kinect. While the investigators may not see anything with their naked eyes, the camera is thought to pick up human-shaped signatures and show them as stick figures on screen.

One such figure has been recorded by an old fire engine, kneeling by the front tires and giving the idea that it was "fixing" something with its movements. Another was filmed in front of a horse-drawn fire wagon "attending" the fake horse that stands at the front of the wagon. And yet another was caught at a desk located just next to the horse-drawn wagon. It almost feels as if the firefighters are still working just as they would have in their respective times.

EVPs (electronic voice phenomena) have been caught by investigators as well. The authors were able to listen to them for themselves, and one was fairly compelling! The investigators can be heard to say, "Is there a fireman in here?" And a hushed masculine voice replies, "Yes, there is one."

Whether the activity in the museum is from firefighters not wanting to stop their important work or from something outside of the building, the Michigan Firehouse Museum believes there may be kindred spirits there that are just as passionate as the staff and volunteers who run the museum to ensure that the history of fighting fires stays strong in our community.

EASTERN MICHIGAN UNIVERSITY

The State of Michigan founded the Michigan State Normal School in Ypsilanti in 1849, making it the first teacher's training school (also called a "normal school") to be opened west of the Allegheny Mountains. On March 29, 1853, the school's first students, 122 in total, began taking classes. Students had to be at least thirteen or fourteen years of age to enroll, depending on which course they were going to specialize in, and all they had to do was pass the entrance exam. No diploma needed—something that may be hard to imagine for modern folks. EMU's own webpage about its history wrote what can only be described as a gut-wrenching description (to people today) of tuition for the times: "Students preparing to be teachers paid $3 per term or $4 for Classics. Those not planning to teach but preparing for college paid $8 a term for Classics and $6 for English." That translates to between $119 and $319 in 2024 dollars. (Commence sobbing, modern students.)

In 1899, when the institution graduated from specializing in secondary education to offering a four-year degree program, the first normal school in the United States to do so, the name was changed to the Michigan State Normal College. By 1939, students were living in on-campus dorms for the first time. The name changed again in 1956 to Eastern Michigan College. After the establishment of the graduate school in 1959, the name changed once again to what it is known as today, Eastern Michigan University (EMU). Unfortunately, none of the original buildings from the original Normal School remains.

Neither do the orchards that once made up the Starkweather farm or the burial grounds that existed where the dorms on the east side of campus stand now. For a more thorough exploration into the cemetery and possible burial

Aerial photo of Michigan State Normal College. *Ypsilanti Historical Society*.

ground that occupied the land before the students did, see the interlude on Ypsilanti's cemeteries in this book.

EMU is home to five colleges and, as of 2022, just over fourteen thousand students. And you better believe there is a ton of campus lore!

Dorm Stories

Every university has its stories of haunted dormitories. A student, usually a young woman, died under mysterious, or sometimes truly gruesome, circumstances, and now rather than move on to whatever awaits her, her soul continues to roam the halls of her former college dorm. Rarely is this alleged spirit malicious. Sometimes she plays harmless tricks, but not often are the students on the receiving end of this activity amused.

Many stories have been posted to the internet over the years, with future, current and past students all throwing in their creepy tales from their times in the dorms. One student had quite the experiences more than a decade ago. In Best Hall, a loud, masculine voice woke them from a dead sleep several times. No one was in their room. Their roommate experienced things as well. In the same Best Hall dorm, they left wadded-up sweatpants on their desk and left to shower, locking the door behind them. (If you are familiar with dorms, you'll know that a lot of them have shared bathrooms on each floor, so you have to leave your room to bathe. It's an enlightening experience to say the least.) When the roommate returned, the sweatpants were folded neatly on the back of the desk chair. According to the original poster, they had not entered the room and done this. If it was a ghost, what a helpful one!

In Downing Hall, these same roommates again experienced odd things. The storyteller described hearing their roommate in bed, tossing and breathing deeply as if asleep…only to see said roommate walk into the room ten minutes later! They also frequently felt someone sitting at the foot of their bed, watching them sleep. Talk about creepy.

But that isn't the only haunting in Downing, where the name Estelle is infamous. The story goes that she was a student who fell to her death from a dorm window. "Former building director Marcius Brock knows her legend well," wrote Karen Joseph in an *Ann Arbor News* article from 1996. "'Estelle,' he said, recalling, 'is a poltergeist, traumatized by the fact that she is not going to a higher world or a lower world.'" Residents of the fourth floor of Downing described a mischievous spirit, being locked in and out of their rooms, doors opening on their own and the elevator seeming to have a mind of its own, moving between floors without anyone calling it.

Liz Hornyak, in her 2019 Halloween article for the campus paper, the *Eastern Echo*, wrote about another pair of roommates who had their fair share of hauntings back in 2007, although they don't name the building. "During their time in the freshman dorms, the girls encountered the spirit of a man that would often manifest to glare at them. They also claim that they were subjected to disembodied voices, finding belongings not where they should be and a radio clock that would blare music when it wasn't plugged in."

There's enough stress on students freshman year as it is without ghosts causing a ruckus. But add in these kinds of shenanigans, and these students are put through the wringer!

Starkweather Hall

EMU's Starkweather Hall was dedicated on March 26, 1897, as the gathering place for the Students' Christian Association of the State Normal, a group that was initially organized in 1881. Mary Ann Starkweather, the building's namesake, donated enough money to the SCA for the hall's construction. More than a century later, Starkweather Hall is now the oldest building on campus.

Starkweather Hall, circa 1895. *Ypsilanti Historical Society*.

Mrs. Starkweather (as she is commonly known) stipulated that the building be used for religious purposes, but the Office of Religious Affairs closed in 1976. Since then, it has served various university functions, serving for a time as the Honors College. Legend has it that Mrs. Starkweather was upset that her intention for the building was no longer honored and now angrily haunts its halls. According to the university's publication, the *Eastern Echo*, Mrs. Starkweather specified that the building be used for religious purposes for one hundred years. As the university fell short of this by twenty-three years, Mrs. Starkweather is upset that her wishes were not upheld.

The basement seems a particular target of activity. A janitor claimed that once while he was there working alone, he felt touched by something he could not see. A shadowy woman dressed in old-fashioned clothing has also been seen. And lights in the basement were known to turn themselves on and off.

Brian Anderson, a longtime employee who worked in the hall, told the *Eastern Echo* in 2009 that the alleged spooky activity is more likely due to rodents making noise in the attic. He also indicated a picture of Mrs.

Starkweather in which it appears horns are growing out of her head, saying, "We try to perpetrate this legend with this picture of Mary Starkweather in the hall that seemed to have grown horns....We [employees] all kind of embellish on this to make the place look haunted."

Whether or not Mrs. Starkweather, rodents or something else is to blame, the "haunted hall" is a popular and enduring campus legend.

Pease Auditorium

Frederic Henry Pease was a beloved EMU professor of music and chairman of the music department. He worked for the college from 1863 until his death from heart failure in 1909. He was laid to rest at Highland Cemetery, where you can visit his grave. Professor Pease had always wanted an auditorium on campus, but his wish was not granted until six years after his death. Pease Auditorium opened in 1915.

But it seems that he may not have left campus entirely, at least according to legend. "In 1980, now-legendary newspaper designer Tim Harrower was then the enterprising editor of the university's student newspaper, the *Eastern Echo*. He wrote a piece of historical fiction in the school's humor magazine, *Spectrum*. His epic saga about the ghost of Pease [Auditorium], rife with intentional inaccuracies, set ablaze the rumor of an unearthly entity in the historic theater." This piece led to the very popular legend that Professor Pease roams the auditorium named for him. Several students came forward after the story was published to claim they had encounters with a very angry, and very dead, Professor Pease.

Frederic Henry Pease. *Ypsilanti Historical Society*.

But what may be stranger is that this is not the only legend out of Pease Auditorium. According to Tom Ogden in his book *Haunted Colleges and Universities*, two students—a soprano and a trumpet player—fell in love sometime in the early 1900s. They met every day at Pease Auditorium to get lunch together. One day, the trumpet player entered Pease and was surprised to find his girlfriend talking to another man. She waved it off as just being friendly, but as the two got to know each other more, the boyfriend grew increasingly jealous. And then one afternoon he found them in Pease, alone. She was singing for the man, something that up until then she had only done for him, her boyfriend.

Having first spotted the pair from the balcony, the trumpeter crept down into the first row of seats and pulled out a gun. He shot both his girlfriend and the new man before turning the gun on himself. Students say that they have heard footsteps on the stairs up to the balcony as well as witnessed one of the chairs in the first row of seats lower by itself, as if someone is sitting down in it.

But there is another version of the story, as told by the event coordinator of Pease, Michael Candy, a junior in 1996. It was not the boyfriend, but his girlfriend who accused him of cheating and shot him. And the trumpeter had a name: Edgar "Zoot" Jackson, who played with the King of Swing. And this apparently happened during a concert in 1947. Jackson died right there on stage.

Candy told the *Ann Arbor News* about hearing doors slam when he was alone in the building, as well as hearing who he described as the ghost of Pease giving an "anguished moan."

While these stories may not have any real truth to them, folks have been and are still experiencing things inside Pease. Whether it's rodents, as is believed to be the case in Starkweather Hall, or something else entirely, there seems to be something odd going on in the old auditorium. Whether or not it is the man for which the auditorium is named is still up in the air. Perhaps EMU would be open to having the hall investigated so the truth of the matter can be found. Or at least there will be some new ghost stories for students to tell.

YPSILANTI STATE HOSPITAL

Although the Ypsilanti State Hospital is no longer standing, its stories remain very much alive in the minds of locals. One famous tale was even brought to the silver screen in 2017, directed by Jon Avnet and starring Peter Dinklage, Richard Gere, Walton Goggins and Bradley Whitford (more on that later).

In 1929, the Michigan government allotted $7.5 million (the equivalent of approximately $135 million in 2023) for the construction of a new "psychopathic hospital" to be located just outside Ypsilanti, to be designed

A postcard of the Ypsilanti State Hospital. *Ypsilanti Historical Society.*

by famed Detroit architect Albert Kahn. Construction began in the summer of 1930, and the hospital opened the following year. Only a few years later, it was already in need of expansion. By 1947, the *Ann Arbor News* was reporting that the Ypsilanti State Mental Hospital was among the "largest and best-equipped institutions of its kind" with "an average population of about 3,500 inmates."

While medical treatment throughout the twentieth century was not as sophisticated as it is today (to put it mildly), patients were given up-to-date medical care—and yes, that did include lobotomies. They also enjoyed special events like on-site carnivals, parades and, after the construction of the auditorium, music and theater performances. Residents were sometimes employed as part of their therapy, paid by the hour, working on menial tasks for the auto industry and creating textiles. They were also, however, used as guinea pigs in experimental medical trials, such as when University of Michigan doctors Thomas Francis Jr. and Jonas Salk worked together to invent the first effective flu vaccine. Luckily, there were no fatalities, and thanks to the inoculated eight thousand residents of the Ypsilanti State Hospital and the Eloise Hospital for the Insane, located in nearby Westland, Michigan, we benefit from their research today. Dr. Salk, who was not often popular with his colleagues, went on to create the first effective polio vaccine, though not without controversy of its own.

Around that same time, a social psychologist named Dr. Milton Rokeach conducted a very different experiment at the Ypsilanti State Hospital. Three patients diagnosed with paranoid schizophrenia—Clyde Benson, Joseph Cassel and Leon Gabor—all believed that they were Jesus Christ. Hoping to cure them of their delusions, Dr. Rokeach brought the men together to see what would happen. The controversial study began on July 1, 1959, and lasted about two years. Dr. Rokeach wrote about the experience in his book *The Three Christs of Ypsilanti*, published in 1964, which was later translated into a stage play, two operas and the not entirely accurate aforementioned film directed by Jon Avnet. In addition to observing the men's interactions, Dr. Rokeach manipulated them in ways criticized by his graduate student assistants. Rather than being freed from their delusions, the men simply regarded the others as fakes. Dr. Rokeach eventually concluded, "[The experiment] did cure me of my godlike delusion that I could manipulate them out of their beliefs."

When former Michigan governor John Engler drastically cut funding to state hospitals in 1991, the Ypsilanti facility's days were numbered. Over the next decade or so, as psychiatric hospitals across Michigan closed one after the other, patients were discharged with punishing results that the state still grapples with years later. Community health agencies were not equipped to care for the influx of severely ill patients, and many still aren't. Countless former hospital residents were left to live on the streets, themselves completely unprepared for such conditions. Many died.

The Ypsilanti Regional Psychiatric Hospital, as it was then called, was one of the first to close its doors, although the Center for Forensic Psychiatry remained open on the hospital's campus until 2001. This is when the slow demolition of the buildings began, starting with administration, the laboratory and the A wards. In 2005, the site was entirely cleared, becoming the new home of the Toyota Technical Center.

Before it was completely gone, however, the former state hospital was a popular destination for urban explorers. People claimed to hear unearthly moans in the desolate buildings as well as experience feelings of unease. The now defunct *Grand Rapids Paranormal Investigation* blog claimed that there was a "satanic room" with a pentagram drawn on the floor and quotes from H.P. Lovecraft written on the walls. Many who explored the abandoned tunnels insist on having had experiences they can only explain by declaring the property haunted.

According to Conner Gossel, host of the *Haunted Historian* podcast, dark figures were seen outside what was once the hospital's walls. "Nobody can say

Ypsilanti State Hospital in disrepair in the 1950s. *Ypsilanti Historical Society*.

for sure who these people [were]," he said, "but many believe them to be the apparitions of the men and women made to leave and die." Gossel also said that before it was torn down, disembodied voices were heard, and a "black mass" would follow anyone daring to explore the abandoned structures.

It is not known if phantom moans and voices continue at the modern Toyota facility. But one thing is for certain. The memories of their unique and varied experiences at the old hospital remain very much alive in the minds of urban explorers as well as former patients and their families. Not to mention the immortalization by Dr. Rokeach and Hollywood of the three Christs of Ypsilanti.

GEDDES AND LEFORGE ROADS

The Michigan Murders

The name John Norman Collins is no longer widely known in the college town of Ypsilanti, but there was a time when his name covered every newspaper headline and was heard in every whisper. He is the serial killer responsible for the "Michigan Murders," heinous killings committed in the Ann Arbor/Ypsi area in the late 1960s. Collins murdered up to eight women, mostly from this area, and left their mutilated bodies within a fifteen-mile radius in Washtenaw County. Two of his "hiding" spots were on LeForge and Geddes Roads.

John Norman Collins shortly after his arrest. *Ypsilanti Historical Society*.

Between 1967 and 1969, John Norman Collins killed up to eight women in both Michigan and California. By all accounts, Collins was a good student and even a star athlete. He was a handsome young man who attended Central Michigan University in Mount Pleasant, Michigan, before transferring to Eastern Michigan University in Ypsilanti. He rode a motorcycle and seemed to have decent luck with the ladies.

Mary Fleszar, only nineteen years old, was found just off LeForge Road in August 1967 in an old farmhouse. The clothing from another of his victims, Dawn Basom, was found in the same farmhouse. Her body, however, wasn't found until 1969. Both women, in fact all of the women connected to Collins, were severely beaten, dismembered and sexually assaulted.

Collins was questioned by police early into his killing spree, but they foolishly concluded that "he just didn't fit the profile of a killer." So, he was set aside as the police continued looking for the type of person they believed capable of committing these heinous crimes, leaving Collins to continue murdering women. He wasn't arrested until after the slaying of Karen Sue Beineman, whose mutilated and assaulted body was found along Huron River Parkway. Even then, it took hair clippings from the crime scene compared to hair from the home Collins was staying at for him to be officially arrested.

Even then, perhaps the strangest part of the entire case was Peter Hurkos, a Dutch psychic, who was hired by a "citizens committee" to come to Michigan to help police find the killer after a multiple of Collins's victims were found. Hurkos, who said he gained psychic powers after falling off a ladder in 1941, was met with a large dose of skepticism by police. But without anything better at the time of his arrival, officers said they would "accept

LeForge Road at Geddes Road, where Collins left the body of Mary Fleszar. *Kay Gray*.

help from anyone" in regards to working with him. And Hurkos actually delivered. He provided police with enough relevant information that they agreed to keep working with him to solve the murders after his initial trial week was up. Hurkos was able to give them the name of a prime suspect whom he shouldn't have known about, and it seems that his "vibrations" led investigators to several new leads in the case. Hurkos further proved himself to officers by touching the closed folder of one of the victims, reenacting a pose from photos inside and naming several of the objects in the photos.

John Norman Collins was arrested on July 31, 1969. He maintained his innocence throughout the entire ordeal and even now claims that he is innocent of his crimes. He was sentenced to life in prison and resides far away from Ypsilanti in Marquette Branch Prison.

At the time of his trial, Collins was only convicted of one murder, that of Karen Sue Beineman. But as technology gets better and as Collins gets older, more and more evidence is being unveiled against him in the deaths of the other women. DNA now tested and letters written by Collins to his cousin in Canada are stacking up against him. He has yet to give a verbal confession to any of the remaining murders, but it may just be a matter of time.

As you head north on LeForge these days, you pass a long row of apartments, mostly full of Eastern Michigan University students, and make a sudden turn into farmland. All that's left standing is a dilapidated silo near the road. The farmhouse was burned down by an unknown arsonist during Collins's murder spree. The silo is covered in vines and graffiti, but it is still an imposing structure and stands over the road that some say is incredibly haunted.

The rumor goes that if you drive down this stretch of road at night, where the farmhouse used to be, the trunk of your car mysteriously pops open. But not only that, if you're lucky (or perhaps unlucky), you'll see the apparitions of a woman, possibly Mary, *and* the old farmhouse. It's not often that buildings are part of a ghostly encounter, but perhaps you'll spot it the next time you take a drive through the area. One Ypsilanti resident the authors spoke to claimed to have seen the female apparition and now refuses to drive down LeForge after dark. She said that the site is most active after 11:00 p.m. or midnight.

However, that is not the only specter in this area. On Geddes, it's said that the ghost of a nurse walks down the side of the road. When you look in your rearview mirror, she's no longer there. The story behind it is that a nurse was killed while walking to the hospital close by (St. Joseph Mercy), but there isn't any evidence to corroborate this legend. Either way, someone or something has made itself known to passersby.

These hauntings share many similarities with others all around the world. Perhaps the most famous in the United States is known as Resurrection Mary, who haunts Archer Avenue in Chicago. All of these apparitions are seen alongside roads. They are usually white in color or sometimes seen as more blue and, very occasionally, red. They repeat the same actions over and over, walking down the same stretch of road and, as in the case of Resurrection Mary, getting into people's cars for a time. A lot of times they have the name Mary, too, although Ypsilanti's own Mary Fleszar was certifiably living, which is not often the case for these so-called Ladies in White.

Ben Goldman of Afterlife Road Productions and another investigator had their own eerie experience on LeForge Road. They were casually investigating, one could say, just checking the road out, seeing if any further investigation may have been warranted. Nothing happened for a while, and it felt like just a regular night, until their spirit box let out a "blood-curdling scream," Ben said. "And then we got a voice that didn't sound like it was coming through the spirit box in the moment." The voice told them to "be careful."

Creeped out, but not so much that they left, Ben and the other investigator went into the bushes to try a pendulum session, which can be used similarly to a Ouija board. They could not be seen from the road. They had just begun asking questions in relation to the murders, wondering if Mary or any of Collins's other victims were still there. "And then this big, white minivan with tinted black windows suddenly speeds down where we are, and comes right up to us, shining its headlights in our eyes. And it says, 'You gotta get out of here.' And then drives away. Just all of a sudden. It was impossible to know we were there. There was no one in the car and we were like, 'Okay, that's weird.'"

They started for their car, not wanting to ignore the warnings from both the spirit box and the mysterious van, but that wasn't the end of the encounter with the strange. A different car turned onto LeForge. "Suddenly this guy is coming from the opposite direction, speeding down the road. And it's like a freaking horror movie. We start running back, and my friend trips! We get off [the road]. And then we get to our car and the car just speeds past us. He doesn't care. But then a bunch of coyotes are howling! We left, and it was just weird. We felt like we were stopped. Someone was following us to [make sure we] leave."

Maybe if you take a drive down Geddes or LeForge after midnight, you, too, can witness the legend for yourself. But remember to take a friend. One should never wander into high strangeness alone.

Bennett Castle

Among all the extravagant and elegant homes found along Geddes Road sits a concrete castle built by one of Michigan's most infamous historical figures. Harry Bennett was the head of Henry Ford's "Service Department," a glorified gang of union busters. Along with killing and wounding employees after the March 7, 1932 Hunger March, Bennett and his gang caused one of the biggest conflicts between unionizers and busters. According to the Detroit Historical Society, the "'Battle of the Overpass' [occurred] on May 26, 1937. On that day, Walter Reuther and other union organizers…arrived to distribute pro-union organizing leaflets at the pedestrian overpass to Gate 4 of the Ford Rouge Plant on Miller Road. While posing for a picture on the overpass, Bennett and as many as 40 members of the Service Department came up behind the union men and beat them severely. No charges were filed."

As one might imagine, Bennett made a lot of enemies, including the Detroit mob. Reportedly, this caused him to be extremely paranoid. (Who can blame him?) This can be seen in the architecture of his very unique home. "Towers, tunnels, spiral staircases, 'switch' steps, secret doors, hidden rooms and many other unique security features were incorporated into its design, all to protect the Lord of the [manor] from 'well wishers,' union men and Detroit gangsters," noted the Henry Ford Heritage Association. This building is made entirely of concrete, with tunnels underneath going to a billiard room where "Ford business" was done, as well as to the "stables" where Bennett kept lions and tigers. (Just in case, you know?) Bennett even built a small "cabin" along Geddes between LeForge and Prospect Roads in case his castle was ever compromised. It came complete with a lookout, gun ports and an underground bunker. Bennett also built several other homes around Michigan and one in Palm Springs, California. All came with the trappings of someone seriously worried about being attacked.

The mysteries surrounding Bennett and these buildings may be small, but they are curious all the same. The first is what else Bennett may have built that no one knows about. The second is what happened to the cabin and underground bunker. The last comment about it comes from a 2015 blog post asking people to stay off the property. The third is what, exactly, killed Harry Bennett.

Gregory Fournier, author of several books on Michigan's odd and eerie past, wrote, "In 1973, Bennett suffered a stroke. In 1975, he entered the Beverly Manor Nursing Home in Los Gatos, California. On January 4, 1979, he died. His death went unreported for a week—the cause was never released to the public."

While the delay of the report was most likely due to his family needing to be notified first, it is still strange that someone so notorious would not get a follow-up. Bennett was older and had suffered a stroke, but the public never learned for sure what sent him to the grave. He did have many enemies. But in the modern day, there are still several of these bizarre monuments to Harry Bennett, and hopefully they will continue standing for years to come, as a reminder of the people who fought for workers' rights more than for those who seek to destroy them.

Please be aware that all of Bennett's former properties are still privately owned. Do not trespass. Always ask permission before exploring.

BONE HEADS BBQ

Since 2009, Bone Heads BBQ has been a popular place for Ypsilantians to sink their teeth into genuine on-site smoked barbecue and other comfort foods. (Do not overlook the homemade macaroni and cheese or the cornbread!) Owned by Jim and Nikki LaChance, the restaurant is located in the unincorporated community of Willis, which was not established until the late 1800s. The building in which Bone Heads resides is older than the village. The current owners believe that it was constructed in 1865, and it has operated as several different businesses over the past century and a half. Per the restaurant's website, it has been "a coach stop, grainery, butcher shop, ice house, post office and general store."

In the 1980s, the building was restored to look like the old general store, making use of "antiques, walnut cabinets and oak trim [that] were brought here from parts of southeastern Michigan and northwest Ohio." It then operated as the Pickle Barrel Inn until ownership changed hands and Bone Heads BBQ was born.

The owners and employees are well aware of their haunted reputation. So many articles have been written about Bone Heads' ghosts, and so many paranormal investigators have been there, that there is a plethora of stories to choose from. And there seems to be an equal number of spirits hanging around that are more than willing to show themselves for employees and visitors alike.

Per the *Ann Arbor News*, "[Nikki] LaChance reports three ghosts haunt Bone Heads. Several employees and guests have seen a woman…in her 40s, while others witnessed an apparition appearing to be a younger girl in her teens. Still other guests have stopped the LaChances to ask why there's a cat in the living room. The only problem is the cat, 'Pickles,' died years ago and is buried underneath the steps on the building's west side." Several visitors have also heard a cat meowing while they are sitting on the patio. The meow sounds like it is coming from within the walls, at about head height. But one bartender, who confessed to being fairly "desensitized" to the paranormal, said, "This is an old building. There could be actual holes in the walls a cat could get into."

The older ghost the LaChances and employees have dubbed "Nellie." Dressed all in white, she has been seen descending the stairs in the dining room. They believe she lived in the building in the early twentieth century and may be the mother of a blacksmith who died on the train tracks near their home. The teenage girl apparition that appears may have come with an

Bone Heads BBQ in early 2024. *Kay Gray.*

antique apothecary cabinet that was brought into the restaurant and dates back to the mid-1800s. But no one has been able to figure out why she is attached to the cabinet or what she is doing in the restaurant. But at least one of these ladies likes to make herself seen to employees and customers alike, both in the dining room and, of course, the ladies' bathroom, a surprisingly common location to find paranormal activity in public spaces. Once, a girl using the women's restroom looked into the mirror only to see a face that was not her own. And another young girl had the lights turn off on her. She also had an eerie feeling both in and around the bathroom. Employees confessed to avoiding the back hallway that leads to the bathroom as much as possible due to this unsettling sensation. Those who use the women's bathroom tend to not look into the mirror if they can help it.

And that's not even half of it. Employees have had items "kicked" back to them after they've dropped them on the floor, lamps in the bar will swing around on their own, bulb ornaments have exploded in front of them and a vase floated through the air all on its own before crashing to the floor. Not to mention the physical feelings employees occasionally have. Invisible fingers brush through their hair, and hearing whispers when no one else is around is not uncommon. Phantom footsteps, lights going on and off (even when the restaurant is closed) and even a ghostly specter washing the upstairs windows have been heard or witnessed at this popular and delicious BBQ joint.

One bartender told of an investigation group with several mediums that came at the end of 2023, which was particularly interesting. The mediums reiterated the names "Jim" and "Sarah" several times, although the bartender didn't know anyone they could have been referring to. He did say that the mediums spent most of their time in the back corner of the building. This happens to be where the women's bathroom is located, as well as the staircase that Nellie can be seen descending.

Crysta visited Bone Heads BBQ with her husband in 2013. There were no supernatural experiences outside of the women's restroom having a distinctly creepy vibe—that could have come from all of the cross-stitch, cherubs, prayers and fake greenery that decorated the stalls. The men's room was an entirely different story, with walls covered in what appeared to be vintage advertisements for syphilis cures and prostitution licenses. Quite the decorative choices! Kay and her husband visited Bone Heads BBQ in January 2024, but nothing supernatural was encountered, other than the restaurant's mouthwatering beef brisket and delicious cornbread.

WILLOW RUN AIRPORT AND YANKEE AIR MUSEUM

Today, Willow Run Airport functions predominantly as a cargo hub for Metro Detroit. (The Detroit Metro Airport is ten miles due east of Willow Run.) It was designed by the famed revolutionary architect of Detroit, Albert Kahn. The Yankee Air Museum operates out of one of its hangars.

Before Willow Run was home to runways or even churning out B-24 Liberators (more on them later), it was Camp Willow Run, a boys' summer camp opened by Henry Ford located on 975 acres of farmland. The name Willow Run comes from the creek that once ran through the property, which contained an apple orchard and fields of soybeans.

Like many people of his day, Henry Ford was an isolationist and not enthused about building airplane motors to support Great Britain in what would become known as World War II. Why would he ruin perfectly good farmland for a war that the United States was not, at the time, personally involved in? Ford himself was an anti-Semite to boot.

However, Ford did agree that should the need arise, and the United States did become involved in the war, his automotive company would produce airplanes, and thus the Willow Run Bomber Plant was born in 1941. The plant was staffed by a great number of women and is considered one of the

The brand-new B-24 bombers at Willow Run. *Ypsilanti Historical Society.*

birthplaces of Rosie the Riveter. (Today, the Yankee Air Museum maintains a Rosie the Riveter Drill Team to raise awareness and represent the museum.) It boasted the creation of the B-23 Liberator, although the plant suffered greatly during wartime. Employees had a very hard time switching from automotive manufacturing to producing aircraft, not to mention that due to the rationing of gasoline and rubber, travel to and from the plant was extremely difficult. To quote from Wikipedia, "In one month Ford had hired 2900 workers but had lost 3100. Ford officials were as a rule anti-union, and Willow Run experienced one serious strike." However, Willow Run carried on. It switched to producing B-24s in 1943. By the end of the war, 8,685 B-24 Liberators had been built at Willow Run.

The B-24 flew further, higher and faster than its B-17 predecessor and was integral to the Allied victory in Europe, seeing action in every corner of the globe. The B-17 Yankee Lady is in the Yankee Air Museum's collection alongside several other combat planes.

After the war, Willow Run became a passenger terminal and the principal airport for Detroit. In 1947, the airport was sold to the University of Michigan for one dollar. Michigan performed many kinds of aeronautical tests and even had a supersonic wind tunnel. Passenger air traffic ceased in

1966 and transferred over to Detroit Metro Airport, making it the area's principal airport. Willow Run was again sold for one dollar to Wayne County in 1977. According to the Detroit Historical Society, "Most of the plant was demolished in 2014 but a 175,000 foot portion was offered to the Yankee Air Museum."

The Yankee Air Museum was established in 1981 and first offered rides in a host of aircraft, including a B-17 Flying Fortress, a B-25 Mitchell Bomber and a C-47 Skytrain. The museum was housed in a hangar at Willow Run. In 2004, a fire destroyed the majority of the museum, save for a few aircraft, and it didn't reopen until 2010. Per the Yankee Air Museum's website, "Following the success of the Save the Bomber Plant campaign, the museum purchased a portion of the Willow Run Bomber Plant that produced B-24 Liberators during World War Two. In 2013, the Museum was able to purchase 144,000 square feet of the Plant. The building is currently being used to house and protect the museum's large aircraft acquisitions." While this was not the entire plant, the museum ensured that at least some of the historic site would not only be preserved but also maintained and used. It has regular events, is open most days of the week and offers memberships!

Willow Run Airport, circa 1971. *Ypsilanti Historical Society.*

Plenty of people over the years have seen or heard strange things in the skies around Willow Run. Mimi Uptergrove related a story about a man named Jeff Westover who reported to the National UFO Reporting Center (NUFORC) that he saw "a barbell-shaped craft comprised of two white spheres connected by a thin bar…[that] revolved horizontally on an axis."

In 2022, Fox News reported people from Lansing to Romulus to Grosse Pointe seeing lights moving through the sky. They were "a silent long thin white line" and made no sound. Photos and video on Fox's website show a long, thin light in the sky, appearing to be incredibly far away. There have been thoughts that it may have been Elon Musk's Starlink satellites, but the eyewitnesses disagree.

Also in 2022, someone filming a practice flight for the Thunder Over Michigan Airshow, held annually at Willow Run, caught something strange in a video taken of the Blue Angels, the feature of that year's airshow. Their report to NUFORC stated, "You can see in the video at the time of filming I noticed something dart away from the aircraft and tried to follow it, but just figured it was a glare or something. Once I broke the video down frame by frame, you can tell the object approaches the plane…then hovers and slightly dips down, then darts up and towards the NE." The object was circular with some kind of haze surrounding it.

To add a little skepticism, an experimental aircraft did crash at Willow Run in 2018, confirming that experimental craft have been tested there in the recent past.

There were strange sightings throughout the 2000s, according to NUFORC. In 2009, an observer spotted an "orange (flame like) light" in the vicinity of Willow Run, ascending into the sky. Thinking it was a balloon, the observer idly watched as it went behind a tree, but they noted that clouds weren't moving and there was no wind at ground level. There was no noise with it, and it headed in a north-northeast direction, toward the airport. It gradually disappeared as it gained altitude. The observer called the local police, Willow Run and 911 to report a possible airplane on fire, but nothing had been reported to any of those agencies.

The sightings of strange things around Willow Run are not just relegated to NUFORC reports, however. Both of the authors have seen odd lights in the area. Both of this book's authors lived in Belleville for a time and, while there, had their own unique experiences.

Crysta's encounter took place while driving home from Ann Arbor one night:

> *I was driving around the bend in 94 where it crosses over Wiard Road heading east. A bright light was hovering in the air south of the highway, on the Rawsonville side, maybe over Belleville Lake, maybe farther off. I had assumed it was somehow an airplane, although it wasn't moving and was extremely bright for a densely cloudy night, going in for a landing at the Detroit Metro Airport. There are about ten miles between Rawsonville and Detroit Metro, and I've seen countless planes land and take off from there—none ever looked like this. Then the light shot off north, toward Willow Run, and disappeared.*

Kay's encounter was more nuanced:

> *It must have been 2012, and it was a cloudy night. I was driving home from one of my jobs after dark. Stuck in traffic at a red light, I was looking around the neighborhood when I noticed multicolored lights in the sky to my left, in the direction of Ypsilanti. They were behind the clouds, undulating in colors of greens, blues and purples. At the time, I presumed them to be the Northern Lights. It was fall, it got dark early, and very occasionally the Lights make their way low enough for us to see them.*
>
> *However, when we began researching this book, and I started looking into Willow Run more closely, and subsequently finding people's UFO reports, not to mention the hauntings in the surrounding areas, I began to question what it was I saw. There were no other reports of the Northern Lights in the area. The news is quick to let folks know. The lights were concentrated in one area—they weren't across the sky. And with how cloudy it was that night, not to mention rainy, I'd be surprised if they could even be seen at all. I don't know what I saw. But after looking into all the weird things people have seen and heard around Willow Run, I'm starting to think those bright, colorful lights weren't the aurora borealis at all.*

She actually had a second encounter six years later, and this time, she wasn't alone:

> *And in 2018, my husband and I saw literal fireballs in the sky above eastern Ypsilanti. We were driving home from the dog park, facing east, and witnessed fifteen to twenty fireballs in the sky, during the evening hours in summer. They disappeared as we drove down Ellsworth Road, one at a time, until our view was obscured by buildings and trees. We immediately checked for lantern festivals or other celebrations in the area and found*

nothing. I have a very terrible photo of the lights on my phone somewhere. There have always been whispers of the strange and futuristic around airports, but with its long, rich, sometimes secretive, history, Willow Run will continue to be talked about by the surrounding community as long as it's a part of Ypsilanti.

Whatever is happening over the skies of Willow Run has a long history. If you find yourself on that side of town, be sure to look up. You never know what you might witness.

THE 1966 UFO SIGHTINGS

If you have ever watched a show on UFOs or done a little reading on them, then you are probably aware of the speculation that they are from "swamp gas" igniting in the atmosphere and appearing as balls of light to the human eye. It's a fairly popular theory still, despite its incredibly sketchy history. But did you know that this idea came from a mass UFO sighting that happened in Washtenaw County in 1966?

March 1966 would turn out to be the month of the flying saucers in southeast Michigan. As early as March 14, sheriff's deputies around Washtenaw County saw something strange in the skies in the wee morning hours. "[The deputies] said there was a single red-green object at first, moving at what were described as 'fantastic' speeds," wrote the *Ann Arbor News* that morning. University of Michigan's alumni publication, *Michigan Today*, wrote in 2014 that Washtenaw deputies said it was "like something out of science fiction. You couldn't believe the thing unless you stood there and watched it." On March 17, deputies at Arkona and Carpenter Roads saw something in the air that "looked like a child's top."

However, the infamous sightings didn't begin there. They came into the spotlight on March 20, 1966, on a farm outside the city of Dexter, which is located about twenty miles northwest of Ypsilanti. Frank Mannor and his son Ronald were in the swamp out behind their farm. What they saw, first on the ground and then up in the sky, stunned them. According to the original article from the *Ann Arbor News*, the thing they saw was about the size of a car and football-shaped with a "quilted" surface. The object was brown in color with four blue-green lights blinking at the right and left edges of it. Periodically it lit up to a yellowish glow, with a light running horizontally

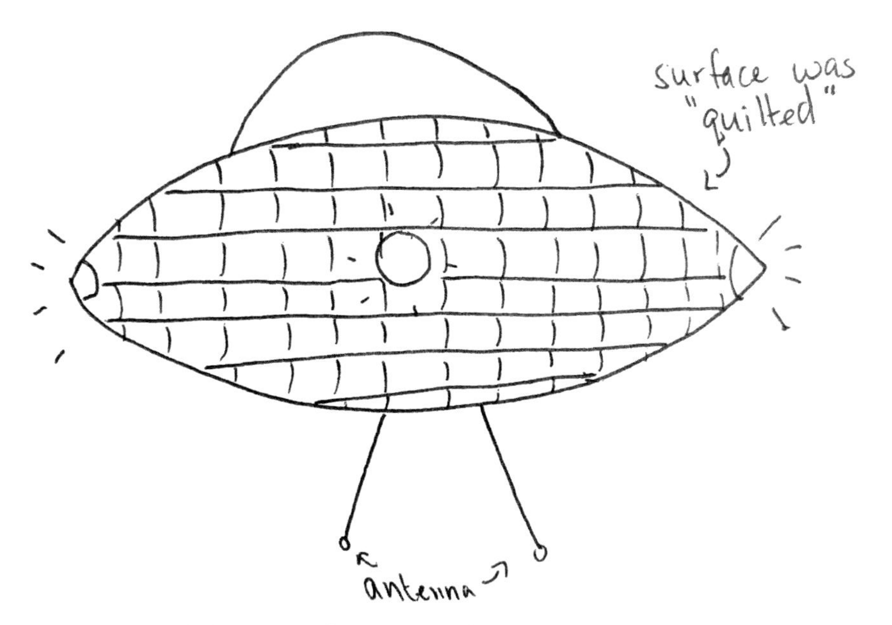

A drawing of the UFO seen over Dexter, Ann Arbor and Ypsilanti based on eyewitness descriptions. *Kay Gray*.

back and forth across the surface of the craft. It was on the ground, but in no time at all, the lights turned bright red, then winked out, and the object went airborne, moving to about five hundred feet farther away from the Mannors. Click on Detroit wrote that after another few minutes of hovering in the air, two "flashlights" shone up at the object. In response, the object shot off across the sky, "whistling…like a rifle bullet ricocheting." All told, the encounter lasted about half an hour.

The Mannors reported the UFO to police, who took their statement, as well as those from about one hundred other folks located all across the county. Washtenaw sheriff's deputies reported seeing moving lights over Lima Township going faster than anything they had ever seen before. Forty miles away in Sylvania, Ohio, police officers were also seeing lights remarkably similar to the ones described in Lima. And fifty miles away, Selfridge Air Force Base in Harrison Township also reported seeing odd lights in the sky that evening in the colors red, green and yellow. But they reported that there were no unfriendly aircraft in the skies above Michigan. Willow Run Airport in Ypsilanti reported the same.

Another witness, Deputy David Fitzpatrick, actually managed to get photos of the mysterious lights. He described the craft as having a blue-green light on top and yellow lights running along the side of it. The deputies watched the lights from around 4:30 a.m. until 7:00 a.m. Two deputies went into the swamp after the lights, chasing it in their patrol car. The lights seemed to follow the contours of the landscape and managed to stay ahead of them despite the terrain and the speed the deputies were driving. The officers lost sight of the lights before a small hill. Once they crested it, the lights were gone.

Two other deputies met them on the other side of that stretch of swamp and asked them if they had seen the lights directly overhead of their (moving) patrol car. The first set of deputies were shocked. They hadn't seen anything above them at all.

On March 21, the night after the Mannor sighting and the pursuit by officers, roughly eighty students at Hillsdale College witnessed strange lights in the sky over their campus, which is located about sixty-five miles southwest of Dexter. The young women in the dorm raised the alarm, calling the head of Civil Defense for Hillsdale College. Unavailable at the time, his wife answered the phone, and she called the police, who responded *several* times that night. The lights that the students witnessed seemed to play with them, disappearing when the police showed up to the college and coming right back once the police left. This happened more than once.

These sightings continued through the twenty-ninth, when two deputies witnessed an object in the sky over the Washtenaw County Jail in Ann Arbor. They gathered other patrolmen and deputies and watched the object for nearly one and a quarter hours. Others in the area saw something similar in both Scio Township and Webster Township. Reports came in from about 7:30 p.m. the evening before until about 4:00 a.m. The object was described as having yellow or orange or brilliant white lights.

All of this activity was just too much to ignore, and it soon attracted the attention of the U.S. government. Project Blue Book was the government's own investigating unit that looked into potential evidence of UFOs. It was led by the astrophysicist (and goatee enthusiast extraordinaire) J. Allen Hynek. Dr. Hynek himself came out to Washtenaw County to see what the heck was going on. He got right to work interviewing anyone and everyone he could find who witnessed the phenomena, but he found the whole scene a total mess. True to form, reporters had already arrived before him (less than twenty-four hours after the Mannors' sighting), swarming like flies around the witnesses and causing confusion.

According to *Michigan Today*, "He found the situation to be one of 'near hysteria,' a media circus attended by hindering crowds of sightseers, thrill-seekers, and the usual assortment of eccentrics. At the Mannors' Dexter farm a man who identified himself as a university professor sat in his car blinking the headlights in Morse code, attempting to contact the supposed aliens. Another man brought a fiddle with which to serenade the UFOs."

Dr. Hynek had a hard time gathering information, partially due to the frenzy swarming Washtenaw County and partly because his jaw was wired shut after a recent surgery. Onlookers and curious folk surrounded the Mannor farm, trampling through the property, teasing and questioning Frank and his son. But Dr. Hynek did manage to gather reports—until his bosses in the government called, not even forty-eight hours after his arrival. Washtenaw County sheriff Doug Harvey said in a 2021 article from the *Sun Times News*, "As soon as we got back to the jail, he had a call from Washington….He went in my office. Twenty minutes later, he comes out of my office, and he says (the press was there), 'We have definitely discovered that it was swamp gas.' Hynek had suddenly gone from 'I really don't know what it is' to 'it was swamp gas' in a matter of minutes," wrote the *Times*. "And that's where it died,' [said] Harvey."

That is where the ever-popular "swamp gas" theory originated. Dr. Hynek held a press conference at the Detroit Press Club Foundation, and while he plainly said that he could not be certain of the actual solution, "marsh gas" was the most likely cause. This, of course, has led to much controversy and discussion. No matter which side of the debate you fall on, it's still pretty cool for Washtenaw County to have been the origin of the theory. Even Walter Cronkite covered the Michigan sightings on his television show *CBS Reports* in an episode titled "UFO: Friend, Foe or Fantasy." The flap was a nationwide sensation!

Apparently, Dr. Hynek forever regretted saying that the UFOs were swamp gas. The "joke" followed him throughout the rest of his life, becoming much more than a brush-off of one event but rather the explanation for sightings for decades to come. He wrote a book much later on in which he described the U.S. Air Force as something of a brick wall when it came to the subject of UFOs: "Once the decision was made that UFOs had to be figments of the imagination, the Air Force policy on UFOs never changed direction. 'It can't be, therefore it isn't' became the guiding principle, and anyone associated with Blue Book, from Director down, learned to follow suit or else."

Frank Mannor also expressed regret, not over having seen the strange craft but for reporting it due to the ensuing mania. He said that if he ever saw the lights or mysterious object again, he wouldn't say a word to anyone. He was threatened and teased and even had his car vandalized. But the world had gotten hold of the sightings, as well as the theory, and it was too late to take it all back.

The UFO sightings of 1966 changed the game for the U.S. government. A Congressional hearing was held about how the government handled not only UFO reports but also transparency to the public. Then congressman from Michigan (and future president) Gerald Ford as well as fellow Michigan congressman Weston Vivian called for a hearing to address these issues. At the time, the U.S. Air Force handled UFO sightings within Project Blue Book, and its response, according to the *Sun Times*, was to brush them all off as nonsense. But the American people wanted more, and they still do. Decades later, "disclosure" is a common phrase among enthusiasts, and another hearing was held by the U.S. government in 2023. But without Dexter, Hillsdale, Dr. Hynek and Representatives Ford and Vivian, strange lights in the sky may have stayed only in the realm of hoaxes and science fiction.

CONCLUSION

Ypsilanti, a place of deep history, has always given off a supernatural feeling, especially at night. Walking through downtown or Depot Town by oneself can feel like a daunting task. The historic buildings, the darkened streets and the characters that make up Ypsi today all add to the mysterious and sometimes eerie air of the city. Knowing that there is probably an old cemetery just around the corner only adds to the mystery. But at the same time, all of these are part of what makes Ypsilanti so enticing.

Learning that there are spirits all over the city and township, and that a good number of them seem to still wander from building to building as if continuing to go about their lives, adds to Ypsi's character, rather than detract from it or make it feel less safe. The people who founded this region of Michigan, who made it what it is, seem to be happy to stick around. If those who saw Ypsi at its beginning are glad to still be here even all these years and decades later, then the city must be doing something right.

Change comes fast and often for a city like this. With so many colleges and universities surrounding it, every year can be completely different from the last. It says something when a town's constant is its ghost population and urban legends. But that doesn't make Ypsi a ghost town—it just makes it a town full of ghosts. And as far as most of this research has uncovered, the ghosts in Ypsilanti don't require saving, or moving on, or are even anything but former residents and visitors who chose not to leave. And that feels, if anything, encouraging.

Hopefully the residents and business owners of Ypsi feel at peace with their spirits, or at least aren't threatened by them. The ghosts have been here all this time, and they probably aren't going anywhere anytime soon. And as Ypsi continues to grow, new stories will be added for future generations to look back on and remember.

Bibliography

Afana, Dana. "Shooting at Ypsilanti Liquor Store Sends Man to Hospital." MLive, 2019. https://www.mlive.com/news/ann-arbor/2019/05/shooting-at-ypsilanti-liquor-store-sends-man-to-hospital.html.

Afterlife Road Productions. "Past Works." 2023. https://www.afterliferoadproductions.com/past-work.html.

Ann Arbor Argus. "Banquet of the U. Of M. Daily." April 7, 1891. Ann Arbor District Library. https://aadl.org/node/100395.

Ann Arbor Democrat. "Dr. W.B. Hinsdale…." September 3, 1897. Ann Arbor District Library. https://aadl.org/node/436446.

———. "The Opera House." September 17, 1897. https://aadl.org/node/436615.

Ann Arbor News. "Dutch Psychic May Get a Cool Reception Here." July 11, 1969. Ann Arbor District Library. https://aadl.org/aa_news_19690711-pg15-dutch_psychic_may_get_cool_reception.

———. "Grand Jury Ordered in Streicher Case." August 20, 1937. Ann Arbor District Library. https://aadl.org/node/212333

———. "La Forge Heard by Grand Jury." October 5, 1937. Ann Arbor District Library. https://aadl.org/node/212343.

———. "Spotted Again by Police: 'Flying Saucers' Return." March 17, 1966. Ann Arbor District Library. https://aadl.org/node/204706.

———. "Strange Flying Objects Sighted." March 14, 1966. Ann Arbor District Library. https://aadl.org/node/204705.

———. "Ypsilanti State Hospital—A Large Place." November 28, 1947. Ann Arbor District Library. https://aadl.org/aa_news_19471128-ypsilanti_state_hospital.

Ann Arbor Registry. "Normal S.C.A. Dedicates Its New Hall." March 25, 1897. Ann Arbor District Library. https://aadl.org/node/560429.

Anschuetz, Jan. "Frederic Henry Pease, a Man for All Seasons." *Ypsilanti Gleanings* (Spring 2012). https://archive.org/details/ypsilanti_gleanings_2012.1_spring/page/n17/mode/2up.

———. "The River Street Saga Continues: Benjamin and Elvira Norris Follett." *Ypsilanti Gleanings* (Summer 2014). https://archive.org/details/ypsilanti_gleanings_2014.2_summer/page/n5/mode/2up.

Badgerow, Ted. "The Sidetrack Bar and Grill." *Ypsilanti Gleanings* (Fall 2009). https://archive.org/details/ypsilanti_gleanings_2009.3_fall.

Biddle, Kenny. "The Xbox Kinect and Paranormal Investigation." *Skeptical Inquirer*, July 7, 2017. https://skepticalinquirer.org/exclusive/the-xbox-kinect-and-paranormal-investigation.

Bien, Laura. "Cemeteries Found on EMU Campus." *Ypsilanti Gleanings* (Fall 2013). https://archive.org/details/ypsilanti_gleanings_2011.3_fall/page/n11/mode/2up.

———. "In the Archives: Woodlawn Cemetery." *Ann Arbor Chronicle*, November 1, 2013. https://annarborchronicle.com/2013/11/01/in-the-archives-woodlawn-cemetery/index.html.

Bingham, Emily. "These 11 Michigan Ghost Towns Are Eerily Intriguing." MLive, October 26, 2016. https://www.mlive.com/travel/2016/10/michigan_ghost_towns.html#2.

Bone Heads BBQ. "History." 2024. https://boneheadsinc.com/history.

Broderick, Claire. Interviewed by Kay Gray and Crysta K. Coburn, January 2024.

Byrne, Kolyn. "Ypsilanti State Hospital—an Abandoned Asylum in Michigan." World Abandoned, June 22, 2021. https://www.worldabandoned.com/ypsilanti-state-hospital.

Cabansag, Ronia-Isabel. "Halloween 2019: Ghosts of EMU." *Eastern Echo*, October 31, 2019. https://www.easternecho.com/article/2019/10/halloween-2019-ghosts-of-emu.

Cabinet Magazine. "The Most Phallic Building in the World" (2003). https://cabinetmagazine.org/events/phallic/winner.php.

CBS. "History Lives—1966: The Year UFOs Came to Michigan." YouTube. 2017. https://www.youtube.com/watch?v=2DjOl1EYgt0.

Chase, Dennis. "Identification Of Suspect Is Claimed For Hurkos." July 24, 1969. *The Ann Arbor News*. https://aadl.org/node/235696.

Cinema Treasures. "Wuerth Theater in Ypsilanti, MI." https://cinematreasures.org/theaters/9694.

City of Ypsilanti Community and Economic Development. "Historic Downtown Walking Tour." Digital, slide show. https://www.cityofypsilanti.com/DocumentCenter/View/2619/Historic-Downtown-Walking-Tour.

Cleary College Journal 2, no. 1 (January 1899).

Counts, John. "Ypsilanti Boy Who Died in 80-Year-Old Cold Case Gets a Gravestone." MLive, October 16, 2016. https://www.mlive.com/news/ann-arbor/2016/10/gravestone_dedicated_for_ypsil.html.

Detroit Free Press. "Did Mental Care Policy Cause Deaths?" September 9, 1994, 10.

Detroit Historical Society. "Bennett, Harry." https://detroithistorical.org/learn/encyclopedia-of-detroit/bennett-harry.

———. "Willow Run." https://detroithistorical.org/learn/encyclopedia-of-detroit/willow-run.

Dooley, Greg. "Harry Bennett's Castle." MVictors.com—Michigan Football History, November 17, 2021. https://mvictors.com/bennetts-castle.

Durr, Matt. "Company Fined Over MIOSHA Violations in Worker Death at Historic Ypsilanti Building." MLive, October 21, 2015. https://www.mlive.com/news/ann-arbor/2015/10/beal_construction_services_fin.html.

———. "Man Sentenced in Thompson Block Arson Stopped Paying Restitution, Records Show." MLive, March 20, 2015. https://www.mlive.com/news/ann-arbor/2015/03/warrant_issued_for_man_who_set.html.

———. "Witness of Thompson Block Death: 'I Wish I Would Have Stopped Him.'" MLive, July 20, 2015. https://www.mlive.com/news/ann-arbor/2015/07/witness_at_thompson_block_floo.html.

———. "Worker Dies After Floor Collapse at Ypsilanti's Historic Thompson Block." MLive, May 11, 2015. https://www.mlive.com/news/ann-arbor/2015/05/construction_worker_at_thompso.html.

Eastern Michigan University. "A Brief History of EMU." 2004. https://web.archive.org/web/20080104155406/http://www.emich.edu/walkingtour/hist.htm.

Eastridge, Jen. Interviewed by Kay Gray and Crysta K. Coburn, Ypsilanti, Michigan, 2023.
Edmunds, William P. "The Beginnings of the Ypsilanti Historical Society." *Ypsilanti Gleanings* (April 2001). https://archive.org/details/ypsilanti_gleanings_2002.1_apr/page/n1/mode/2up.
Egeler, Dave, Director of Operations, Michigan Firehouse Museum. Interviewed by Kay Gray and Crysta K. Coburn, Summer 2023.
Employees of Bone Heads BBQ. Interviewed by Kay Gray, January 2024.
Encyclopaedia Britannica. "Ypsilanti | Historic City, Huron River, Eastern Michigan." December 22, 2023. https://www.britannica.com/place/Ypsilanti.
Facebook. "Asa & Minerva Dow." Ypsilanti Historical Society, October 20, 2020. https://www.facebook.com/ypsihistory/posts/asa-minerva-dow-built-what-is-now-our-museum-in-1860-minerva-died-shortly-after-/10158674870434383.
———. "Ypsilanti Area Discussion Group," 2023. https://www.facebook.com/groups/YpsilantiDiscussion.
First Fridays Ypsi. "The Smeet Frog Festival." 2023. https://firstfridaysypsi.com/location/the-smeet-frog-festival.
Fletcher, Foster. "As It Was in the Beginning." *Ypsilanti Gleanings* (February 1975). https://archive.org/details/ypsilanti_gleanings_1975.02/mode/2up.
———. "As It Was in the Beginning (Third Article)." *Ypsilanti Gleanings* (November 1976). https://archive.org/details/ypsilanti_gleanings_1976.11/page/n17/mode/2up.
Fournier, Gregory. "Clinton LeForge Runs Amuck in Ypsilanti." Fornology, July 17, 2017, https://fornology.blogspot.com/2017/07/clinton-leforge-runs-amuck-in-ypsilanti.html.
———. "Henry Ford's Tough Guy—Harry Bennett." Fornology, December 1, 2015. https://fornology.blogspot.com/2015/12/henry-fords-tough-guy-harry-bennett.html.
———. *The Richard Streicher Jr. Murder: Ypsilanti's Depot Town Mystery*. Tucson, AZ: Wheatmark Inc., 2018.
Ghosts of America. "Ypsilanti, Michigan, Ghost Sightings." https://www.ghostsofamerica.com/4/Michigan_Ypsilanti_ghost_sightings8.html.
———. "Ypsilanti, Michigan, Ghost Sightings." https://www.ghostsofamerica.com/4/Michigan_Ypsilanti_ghost_sightings3.html.
The Ghosts of South Lyon and Other Areas. "The Great Big Highland Cemetery, with a Surprising Twist to It." https://ghostsofsouthlyon.blogspot.com.

Glenn, Alan. "Ann Arbor vs. the Flying Saucers." Michigan Today, 2014. https://michigantoday.umich.edu/2014/04/13/ann-arbor-vs-the-flying-saucers.

Goldman, Ben. Interviewed by Kay Gray and Crysta Coburn, January 2024. Back Office Studios, Ypsilanti, Michigan.

Great Lakes Ghost Hunters of Michigan. "G.L.G.H. of MI • Pleasant View/Soop Cemetery, Belleville, MI 8 Dec 2018." December 8, 2018. https://glghmi.com/investigations/2018-investigations/pleasant-view-soop-cemetery-belleville-mi-8-dec-2018.

Guterman, Nan. "Follett House Depot Town, Ypsilanti Michigan." Research paper, 2023.

Haddad, Ken. "'I'll Believe This to the Day I Die': A Look Back at the Michigan UFO Craze of 1966." *All About Ann Arbor*, April 3, 2023. Click On Detroit. https://www.clickondetroit.com/all-about-ann-arbor/2017/03/15/the-michigan-ufo-craze-of-1966.

Haunted.Historian. "In Memoriam Post." Instagram, April 30, 2020. https://www.instagram.com/p/B_m1wNOFOdH.

Heffner, Matt. "25 Most Haunted Places in Michigan | Plan a Haunted Michigan Road Trip." Awesome Mitten, October 11, 2023. https://www.awesomemitten.com/ten-haunted-places-in-michigan.

The Henry Ford. "B-24 Liberator Assembly Line at Ford Willow Run Bomber Plant, 1944." https://www.thehenryford.org/artifact/229817.

Henry Ford Heritage. "A Tough Guy's XANADU: HFHA Members Tour Harry Bennett's Castle." https://henryfordheritage.blogspot.com.

Heritage News. "News from Yesteryear: From the Masonic Temple to the Riverside Arts Center." March 1995. https://yhf.org/wp-content/uploads/YHF_Newsletters_1995.pdf.

———. "Thompson Block: An Interesting Past, a Promising Future?" November 2013.

Hess, Rob, owner of Go! Ice Cream. Interviewed by Kay Gray and Crysta K. Coburn, Ypsilanti, Michigan, 2023.

Hewett, Robert. "Authorities Seek Three in Boy's Death." *Ann Arbor News*, March 11, 1935. Ann Arbor District Library. https://aadl.org/node/212320.

———. "Parents Questioned in Boy's Murder Case." *Ann Arbor News*, March 14, 1935. Ann Arbor District Library. https://aadl.org/node/212324.

———. "'Sex Maniac' Is Sought in Boy's Murder." *Ann Arbor News*, March 9, 1935. Ann Arbor District Library. https://aadl.org/node/212317.

Higgins, Lee. "Large Fire Guts Historic Building in Ypsilanti's Depot Town; Officials Label Fire 'Suspicious.'" *Ann Arbor News*, September 23, 2009. https://www.annarbor.com/news/large-fire-guts-historic-building-in-ypsilantis-depot-town.

Instagram. "SmeetFrog4Ypsi." https://www.instagram.com/smeetfrog4ypsi.

Jones, R.D. "Occidental Hotel & Bathhouse." Michigan Transportation History, 2020. www.michtranshist.info.

Jordan, Tanet. Interviewed by Kay Gray and Crysta K. Coburn, Ypsilanti, Michigan, 2023.

Joseph, Karen. "School Spirit." *Ann Arbor News*, October 27, 1996. Ann Arbor District Library. https://aadl.org/node/203014.

Keister, Douglas. *Stories in Stone : A Field Guide to Cemetery Symbolism and Iconography*. Layton, UT: Gibbs Smith, 2004.

Kenigsberg, Ben. "'Three Christs' Review: Exploring the Mysteries of the Mind." *New York Times*, January 9, 2020. https://www.nytimes.com/2020/01/09/movies/three-christs-review.html.

Kimmer, Retro. "Harry Bennett's Castle." Retro Kimmer's Blog, October, 6, 2009. https://www.retrokimmer.com/2009/10/harry-bennetts-castle.html.

Kirsch, Tom. "Ypsilanti State Hospital Located in Ypsilanti, MI." Opacity: Urban Ruins, October 15, 2014. https://opacity.us/site102_ypsilanti_state_hospital.htm.

Komer, David. "Strange Lights in the Sky Spotted over Southeast Michigan Thursday Night." FOX 2 Detroit, April 22, 2022. https://www.fox2detroit.com/news/strange-lights-in-the-sky-spotted-over-se-michigan-thursday-night.

Lamb, Cyril. "Seven-Year-Old Ypsilanti Boy Murdered." *Ann Arbor News*, March 8, 1935. https://aadl.org/node/212330.

Lasher. "Soop Cemetery." Mysterious Michigan, August 17, 2022. https://mysteriousmichigan.com/soop-cemetery.

LocalWiki. "Look in the Attic." https://localwiki.org/ann-arbor/Look_In_The_Attic.

Lockheed Martin. "The B-24: The Great Liberator." https://www.lockheedmartin.com/en-us/news/features/history/b-24.html.

Mann, James. "The Bones of Bell Street." *Ypsilanti Gleanings* (Spring 2013). https://ypsihistory.org/publications/spring2013.pdf.

———. "The 1893 Cyclone." *Ypsilanti Gleanings* (Winter 2014). https://archive.org/details/ypsilanti_gleanings_2014.4_winter/page/n7/mode/2up.

———. "Ghost Hunting in the Museum." *Ypsilanti Gleanings* (Summer 2009). https://archive.org/details/ypsilanti_gleanings_2009.2_summer/page/n15/mode/2up.

———. "Historic Block Played Many Roles." *Ann Arbor News*, September 27, 2008.

———. "History." St. John the Baptist Catholic Church. https://www.ypsilanticatholic.org/history.

———. Interviewed by Kay Gray and Crysta K. Coburn, Ypsilanti, Michigan, 2023.

———. "Legend of the Smeet Frog." *Ypsilanti Gleanings* (Spring 2014). https://archive.org/details/ypsilanti_gleanings_2014.1_spring/page/n13/mode/2up.

———. "Pettibone Cemetery." *Ypsilanti Gleanings* (Fall 2009). https://archive.org/details/ypsilanti_gleanings_2009.3_fall/page/n13/mode/2up.

———. "The Thompson Block—Then and Now!" *Ypsilanti Gleanings* (Winter 2009). https://archive.org/details/ypsilanti_gleanings_2009.4_winter/mode/2up.

———. "The Towner House—A Diamond in the Rough." *Ypsilanti Gleanings* (Spring 2015). https://archive.org/details/ypsilanti_gleanings_2015.1_spring/page/n7/mode/2up.

———. "Woodlawn Cemetery." *Ypsilanti Gleanings* (Fall 2018). https://archive.org/details/ypsilanti_gleanings_2018.3_fall/page/n23/mode/2up.

Marrin, Doug. "How the Military Cover-Up of the Dexter UFO Incident Led to Greater Government Transparency." *Sun Times News*, March 12, 2021. https://thesuntimesnews.com/g/chelsea-mi/n/25233/how-military-cover-dexter-ufo-incident-led-greater-government-transparency.

Maynard, Mark. "Talking About Highland Cemetery's Starkweather Chapel, and the History of Ypsilanti's Death Industry." December 18, 2019. http://markmaynard.com/2019/12/starkweather-memorial-chapel-at-highland-cemetery.

Metromode. "Ypsi Builder to Renovate Historic Starkweather House." October 18, 2007. https://www.secondwavemedia.com/metromode/devnews/starkweatherypsi0041.aspx.

Military History of the Upper Great Lakes. "The Ford Family at Willow Run." October 12, 2015. https://ss.sites.mtu.edu/mhugl/2015/10/12/the-ford-family-at-willow-run.

Milliman, Doris. "Did You Know?" *Ypsilanti Gleanings* (April 1987). https://archive.org/details/ypsilanti_gleanings_1987.04/page/n11/mode/2up.

Mull, Carol E. *The Underground Railroad in Michigan*. Jefferson, NC: McFarland & Company, 2010.

NUFORC National UFO Reporting Center. "NUFORC Sighting 171729." October 8, 2022. https://nuforc.org/sighting/?id=171729.

———. "NUFORC Sighting 71277." August 5, 2009. https://nuforc.org/sighting/?id=71277.

Ogden, Tom. *Haunted Colleges and Universities: Creepy Campuses, Scary Scholars, Deadly Dorms*. Hoopla ed. Guilford, CT: Globe Pequot, 2014, 122–23.

Oztman, Rosemary K. "Is the Now-Closed Denton Road Bridge a Haunted Place?" *Belleville-Area Independent*, October 13, 2022. https://bellevilleareaindependent.com/is-the-now-closed-denton-road-bridge-a-haunted-place.

Parlette, Noëlle. "Starkweather Hall Surrounded by Haunted History." *Eastern Echo*, October 28, 2009. https://www.easternecho.com/article/2009/10/starkweather_hall_surrounded_by_haunted_history.

———. "Ypsi Tower History." *Eastern Echo*, September 25, 2011. https://www.easternecho.com/article/2011/09/ypsi_tower_history.

Perkins, Tom. "Washtenaw County Spirits Reported to Be Mischievous but Friendly." *Ann Arbor News*, October 24, 2012. https://www.annarbor.com/news/washtenaw-county-spirits-reported-to-be-mischevious-but-friendly.

———. "Ypsilanti to Recognize 'Indigenous Peoples Day' on Columbus Day." MLive, June 23, 2016. https://www.mlive.com/news/ann-arbor/2016/06/ypsilanti_will_recognize_indig.html.

Pety, Gerry. "Really…Again!" *Ypsilanti Gleanings* (Summer 2005). https://archive.org/details/ypsilanti_gleanings_2005.2_summer/page/n9/mode/2up.

Pizzino, Greg. Personal investigation notes. December 2023.

Planet Weird. "We've Been Cursed! Deadly Hexes, Witchcraft, and Mormon Bigfoot | Ep. 017 | Haunted Objects Pod." June 12, 2023. https://www.youtube.com/watch?v=bUVUtvdRxvg.

Plymouth Ghost Hunters. "The Brick & Mortar—Ypsilanti—11 19 22." January 6, 2024. https://www.youtube.com/watch?v=H82WTBR5Sjk.

Random Times. "Elizabeth: The 'Witch' of Union-Udell Cemetery, Ypsilanti—Michigan." August 24, 2020. https://random-times.com/2020/08/24/elizabeth-the-witch-of-union-udell-cemetery-ypsilanti-michigan.

Reddit. "Know of Any Good Campus Ghost Stories?" Post by gtfolmao, October 15, 2012. https://www.reddit.com/r/emu/comments/11jkfm/

comment/c6v4jzh/?utm_source=share&utm_medium=web3x&utm_name=web3xcss&utm_term=1&utm_content=share_button.

Ridenour, George. "Summit Street Cemetery." *Ypsilanti Gleanings* (Spring 2015). https://archive.org/details/ypsilanti_gleanings_2015.1_spring/page/n29/mode/2up.

———. "Was That You, Minerva?" *Ypsilanti Gleanings* (Spring 2007). https://archive.org/details/ypsilanti_gleanings_2007.1_spring/page/n13/mode/2up.

Robinson, John. "Controversial, but Michigan Has Embraced the Ypsilanti Water Tower." 99.1 WFMK, March 31, 2023. https://99wfmk.com/ypsilanti-water-tower.

———. "Haunted Michigan: The Old Whittaker House, Ypsilanti." 99.1 WFMK, September 2, 2022. https://99wfmk.com/whittakerypsilanti.

———. "Haunted Michigan: The Witch of Union-Udell Cemetery, Ypsilanti." 99.1 WFMK, September 11, 2023. https://99wfmk.com/union-udell-cmetery.

———. "The 'Witch' of Soop Cemetery: Belleville, Michigan." 99.1 WFMK, December 5, 2023. https://99wfmk.com/soop-witch-2020.

Robinson, Veronica. "John Burton, One of the First African American Mayors in Michigan." *Ypsilanti Gleanings* (Winter 2008). https://aadl.org/ypsigleanings/19587.

Ross, John. "The Man Who Banished the Iron Lung." *Wall Street Journal*, June 5, 2015. https://www.wsj.com/articles/the-man-who-banished-the-iron-lung-1433537703.

Rudisill, Al. "Highland Cemetery—The Beginning." *Ypsilanti Gleanings* (Spring 2008). Ann Arbor District Library. https://aadl.org/ypsigleanings/15344.

———. "The Ypsilanti Water Tower." *Ypsilanti Gleanings* (Summer 2008). https://archive.org/details/ypsilanti_gleanings_2008.2_summer/page/n3/mode/2up.

Safoutin, Mike. "Old Rawsonville: Setting the Record Straight." What Shall We Weird?, February 2, 2024. https://whatshallweweird.com/1477/old-rawsonville-setting-the-record-straight.

Schultz, Sherri. Interviewed by Kay Gray and Crysta K. Coburn, Ypsilanti, Michigan, Summer 2023.

Snap Judgment. "The Three Christs of Ypsilanti." NPR, May 2, 2014. https://www.npr.org/2014/05/02/309004267/the-three-christs-of-ypsilanti.

Sonnenberg, Mike. "The Haunted Hall in Ypsi." Lost in Michigan, March 29, 2020. https://lostinmichigan.net/the-haunted-hall-in-ypsi.

Thompson & Co. https://www.thompsondepot.com.

Thuma, Cynthia, and Catherine Lower. *Creepy Colleges and Haunted Universities: True Ghost Stories*. Atglen, PA: Schiffer Publishing, 2003.

Treml, William B. "Landing of 'Saucer' Reported." *Ann Arbor News*, March 21, 1966. Ann Arbor District Library. https://aadl.org/node/204708.

Turkawski, Laurie. "The Many Lives of the Ypsilanti Historical Museum." *Ypsilanti Gleanings* (Summer 2007). https://archive.org/details/ypsilanti_gleanings_2007.2_summer/page/18/mode/2up.

Uptergrove, Mimi. *Ann Arbor Area Ghosts*. Atglen, PA: Schiffer Publishing, 2008.

Volunteer at the Ypsilanti Historical Society. Interviewed by Kay Gray and Crysta K. Coburn, December 2023.

Waymarking. "Starkweather Home/Ladies Library—Ypsilanti, Michigan." https://www.waymarking.com/waymarks/WM3DGE.

WEX Definitions Team. "Redlining." Legal Information Institute. https://www.law.cornell.edu/wex/redlining.

Wikipedia. "Dodge." February 6, 2024. https://en.wikipedia.org/wiki/Dodge.

———. "Harry Bennett." January 31, 2024. https://en.wikipedia.org/wiki/Harry_Bennett.

———. "Willow Run Airport." December 2, 2023. https://en.wikipedia.org/wiki/Willow_Run_Airport.

———. "Ypsilanti Water Tower." February 1, 2024. https://en.wikipedia.org/wiki/Ypsilanti_Water_Tower#cite_ref-nris_1-0.

WikiWikiWeb. "Smeet Frog." November 2014. https://wiki.c2.com/?SmeetFrog.

Witsil, Frank. "'Handsome' EMU Student Was Unlikely Serial Killer Suspect. Letters, Interviews Reveal Dark Side." *Detroit Free Press*, December 16, 2019. https://www.freep.com/in-depth/news/local/michigan/2019/11/11/john-norman-collins-michigan-murder-suspects-letters-interviews/2522765001.

World of Rocks employee. Interviewed by Kay Gray and Crysta K. Coburn, Ypsilanti, Michigan, January 2024.

WXYZ Detroit. "Experimental Plane Crashes during Test at Willow Run Airport." December 14, 2018. https://www.wxyz.com/news/experimental-plane-crashes-during-test-at-willow-run-airport.

Yankee Air Museum. "About Us." January 3, 2024. https://yankeeairmuseum.org/about-us.

———. "Aircraft Collection." November 17, 2023. https://yankeeairmuseum.org/aircraft-collection.

———. "Rosie the Riveter." January 18, 2022. https://yankeeairmuseum.org/rosie-the-riveter.

Ypsi Alehouse. "Our Beautiful Brews." 2023. https://ypsialehouse.com/brews.php.

Ypsi Real. "Don't Take Ypsilanti's Parks for Granted, They Haven't Always Been Here." June 23, 2015. https://www.ypsireal.com/blog/post/history-ypsi-parks.

———. "Ypsilanti: What's in a Name?" October 14, 2019. https://www.ypsireal.com/blog/post/history-ypsilanti-name.

Ypsilanti Gleanings. "Ypsilanti's Mineral Water Sanitariums" (February 2, 1973). https://archive.org/details/ypsilanti_gleanings_1973.02/page/n1/mode/2up.

Ypsilanti Historical Society. "About—Ypsi Historical Society." June 9, 2022. https://ypsihistory.org/about.

———. "Historical Markers & Statues—Ypsilanti, Michigan." 2022. https://ypsihistory.org/wp-content/uploads/2022/03/Historical-Markers-and-Statues.pdf.

Zettelmaier, Joseph. "Plays." Joseph Zettelmaier—Playwright. https://www.jzettelmaier.com/plays.html.

Zimmer, Dennis. "The Roman Catholic Church Here Has Almost No History." *Ypsilanti Gleanings* (Fall 2006). https://archive.org/details/ypsilanti_gleanings_2006.3_fall/page/n3/mode/2up.

About the Authors

Crysta K. Coburn has been writing award-winning stories for most of her life. Her first short story was published at the age of sixteen after she won runner-up in a local writing contest. She earned her bachelor's degree in creative writing from Western Michigan University in 2005. She is a fiction writer, poet, playwright, journalist, editor, podcast host and occasional lyricist. She cohosts the popular podcast *Haunted Mitten*. Find her online at crystakcoburn.com.

Kay Gray has been studying the paranormal and supernatural for close to twenty-five years. She is cohost of the popular podcast *Haunted Mitten*, author of several short stories in the steampunk genre and an occasional dramaturge for the Neighborhood Theatre Group. When she is not writing or reading, she can be found lost in nature with her dog and husband. Find her online @kgraywrites on almost all platforms.

Haunted Mitten is a podcast covering all things paranormal in the state of Michigan. Wanting to share their knowledge of the weird and their love of the hand-shaped state, Crysta K. Coburn and Kay Gray decided that a podcast was the best way to get the word out. Crysta and Kay began this journey in 2019 and have five completed seasons with many more to come. Find *Haunted Mitten* at hauntedmitten.com or anywhere one gets podcasts.